Gone Fishin...
for Carp

Gone Fishin'...
for Carp

Manny Luftglass

Gone Fishin' Enterprises
Manny Luftglass T/A Gone Fishin' Enterprises
15 LaJolla South • Annandale, NJ 08801

Gone Fishin' For Carp
By Manny Luftglass

Published By
Gone Fishin' Enterprises
15 LaJolla South, Annandale New Jersey 08801

ISBN: 0-9650261-3-2
UPC#: 7 93380 54821 6

Photo Credits:
"Carp In North America," "Why Fish Carp?," George Harsel, Dave Bank, Iain Sorrell,
Nigel Griffen, Blackwater Sport Center, Dan's Sport Shop, Valley Tackle,
Fairfield Sporting Goods, Tony Broomer, Carp Anglers Group,
as well as author's private collection.

Design & Typography:
TeleSet
Somerville, New Jersey

PRINTED IN THE UNITED STATES OF AMERICA.

Pictured on the cover: *(On the left.)* Your self-appointed New Jersey carp guru, author Manny Luftglass with 13½ pound German carp he put back into Spruce Run Reservoir, New Jersey. And next to him, Tim Paisley, Editor of "CarpWorld," a monthly magazine in the United Kingdom, holding an English leather carp of over thirty pounds.

Pictured on the back: Small carp, big fire. Nightime on the Big "D." Luke Harsel of Flemington, New Jersey about to return a Delaware River Big-Scaler.

Easy enough, I hereby dedicate this book to the countless carp that have given me so many, many hours of glorious pleasure.

It has been a great ride, and I hope to stay on the carp train for quite a few more years to come. You see, I used to think I knew nearly everything there was to know about catching "Mr. Man," but once I sat myself down to put "Gone Fishin' for Carp" together, I realized how little I really did know.

My first three books, "Gone Fishin' in Spruce Run Reservoir," "Gone Fishin' in Round Valley Reservoir," and "Gone Fishin' in N.J. Saltwater Rivers & Bays" took less time combined to write than it took me to put this book together for you. Funny thing, again, I thought I could just sit and type, but after reading about so many folks who do it with more skill, I learned more than I ever thought imaginable. That which I found out about is what I hope to be able to share with you readers now.

Number one in the dedication list is, as stated, all carp, everywhere, those I have caught, missed, and those who await my bait.

Past the fish themselves are a large number of fine people who spent time with me, helping with my research, and the people too who wrote so much about carp angling that I will be sharing with you here ...

When I tell you about a particular location I might refer to a person or two who helped, but separate from that, let me say now that a quartet of Englishmen were truly super!

Phil Lockley, a carp angler who works for a commercial fishing magazine called "Fishing News," called me from England in response to an outreach I shot-gunned to many papers in Britain. Forgive the play on words, Phil, but you helped "Unlock" a lot of information for me. Besides his words about carp angling in England, Phil sent me several of the newspapers that I learned from.

Mark Herbert is the Chief Sports Sub-Editor of the world renowned London Times, and he too gave me a great many details, also sending me lots of reading matter. He spent about a gadillion "Quid" one day with me on the telephone.

Another person from England, now transplanted in Connecticut, Iain Sorrell, helped me translate some words and terms I found in the various English books and magazines I obtained. We think we speak the same language, but while we in America learned pretty well, the "Brit's" came up with lots of new stuff that required English to American translation. We spell many words differently, but that is good for me. If I goof up a word, you might think that it is spelled that way across the pond — one way or the other.

You can buy most of the strange named items we will talk about in the chapter about England from Iain. He can be telephoned at 1-860-673-4274 for a catalog.

In outreaching for photo's for this book, I asked many tackle store proprietors if they had any pictures, and one such person was Al Corry of Fairfield Sporting Goods in Pine Brook, N.J. Rather than sending a photo, Al sent me the real thing, a fellow who walked into his store only a few hours after my call, asking Al if he knew of anyone who fished for carp in New Jersey! Al had Carper Tony Broomer, who had just moved to Lake Hiawatha, N.J. from Bedford, England at the start of 1996, call me, and we visited in person to make sure that I had the translations just right.

I learned a great deal from reading "Why Fish Carp?" written by Dan Gapen Sr., of Minnesota. Also from a book put out by the American Fisheries Society" entitled "Carp in North America," and when we talk about carp in Pennsylvania, you will see that I interviewed the author of this book too, Edwin L. Cooper.

Carp being what they are in England, respected as they should be, I read much of the how-to's, etc., in four periodicals. "CarpWorld" is a magazine edited by Tim Paisley, who clearly must be the only person known to man who absolutely likes to fish for carp more than I do! Another excellent magazine is "David Hall's Advanced Carp Fishing." Two super weekly newspapers are "Angler's Mail," and "Angling Times," and while not solely about carp, they are packed full of great information.

Last but not least, a huge thank you to Ron Bern for his assistance with the "Carp in the Bathtub" chapter, as well as for his writing about South Carolina, but mostly, for just being my friend.

A very long dedication for so small a book, but necessary!

Contents

Foreword

I began to fish for carp at a place that most people never would have thought of as holding any live fish at all! Growing up in Brooklyn, N.Y., home of "A Tree Grows in Brooklyn," and once of the then-called Brooklyn Dodger baseball team, Brooklyn is also where Prospect Park is located! There is a fine zoo at the park, as well as beautiful Botanical Gardens, but my favorite was THE LAKE.

Prospect Park Lake may not exactly be a spot to fish the night through at any longer, unless you come prepared with a body-guard or two, but no doubt it still holds some of the smarter carp on the planet. You have to be way above average to keep afloat in New York City, be you human, or a "Big-Scaler!"

It was at Prospect Park that three of us teenagers got together and decided to head north to fish for carp. The location was the Walkill River, to be discussed in far greater detail later on.

My first weekend on the Walkill was wildly exciting, and still clearly stuck in my brain, even though I did not catch a single carp at all!

We will talk later about how we fished the Walkill, so incredibly rustic a style. Style had nothing to do with my being hooked! What made me a carp fisherman that weekend was one fish, a single carp, and it was not even on my line!

The weekend passed with the three of us getting a few bites, but catching nothing. On Sunday morning, Maurice had a drag-screamer! He picked up the six foot solid glass rod, and stuck the steel. The old Mitchell 300 drag was loud and true, and the line tore away ....

Maurice did everything a human could have done then to stop the fish. He tightened the drag quite a bit, but still the beast swam. Trying another trick, he left slack line, opening the bale, but the carp did not stop swimming, although that stunt works to this day sometimes. Banging on the butt of the rod, sending shock waves through the line, hoping at least to turn the fish, did not do it either.

One hundred yards of brand new eight pound test line peeled away, as quick as that, and the black spool base appeared. Down to the knot, and, SNAP! ... it went.

That was our only hooked carp of the weekend, and it may still be out there somewhere. It made me a carp fisherman for life though, I swear it!

———————

CHAPTER 1

"The Carp In The Bathtub"

Here's a true story about the introduction of a book bearing the above title. The title references a children's book which involved the author in an odd but wholly welcomed role. In fact, my involvement centered around the requirement to catch a carp — to star at a press conference!

The little children's book which is central to this story had its roots in Eastern European customs, transported whole to the United States with the great waves of immigrants about the turn of the century. One such custom was the purchase by Jewish immigrants of live carp several days before the feast of Passover. Often, as the name of the book suggests, the carp were placed in bathtubs filled with water, thereupon to swim and presumably to purge their stomachs of objectionable contents, until such time as they kept their unfortunate appointments with the cook.

The carp were boiled, ground and converted into a strange, glutinous dish called "gefilte fish" which was (and is) served cold, with horseradish hot enough to bring tears to the eyes of the most stalwart Passover Dinner guest. (Fortunately for those of us dedicated to the continued health and well-being of carp, gefilte fish devotees have moved on these days to whitefish, northern pike, yellow perch, sucker and chub as the fish of choice.)

The whole idea of a carp in the bathtub somehow captured the interest of a writer I knew named Barbara Cohen. Barbara was clearly at least one full generation removed from any such experience. However, she had heard about it more than once from her parents, who owned the beautiful Somerville Inn in Somerville, New Jersey.

Perhaps Barbara wondered how she might have reacted to a carp in her own bathtub, were she a child one hundred years ago in some poor "shetl" in Russia or the lower east side of New York. Out of this wondering grew her story about two children who "adopted" the carp that their father brought home and placed in their bathtub, preparatory to the Passover feast. The children in her story go to extraordinary lengths to save the carp, up to and including an especially creative exercise in kidnapping ("fishnapping?") I won't reveal the ending, since the book is still in print and your children — regardless of nationality or ethnic origin — would love it as a gift.

Barbara completed the text and her friend, Joan Halpern, an artist, developed the illustrations and the book went to press. Several days before a scheduled press party to introduce "The Carp in the Bathtub," I happened to be dining at the Somerville Inn where Gene Cohen, Barbara's husband, joined me at my table. He told me about the book and the imminent press party and asked if I could catch a carp.

"Could I catch a carp"? I asked rhetorically, thinking as I did what a musical sound rang in those words, what pleasures they portended, as did every prelude to each and every carp expedition I could recall. It was summer, the great Delaware River was running clean and well within its banks, and God was in His heaven. Of course I could catch a carp.

"But for what purpose?"

Gene explained that he and Barbara were planning a party to introduce the book right here in the Inn and they planned to have a large antique bathtub, complete with raised legs, water, and a live carp (if I could oblige them) as the centerpiece of the affair.

I promised Gene that I would indeed oblige them. It was only after he left the table that I began to consider that I had left myself no room for error, since there was only one fishing day before the party. There are days when the best efforts of even the most skilled and determined anglers produce no carp; days when we grumble to our fishing partners about phases of the moon and falling barometers and depleted oxygen levels and solunar tables;

days when the best we can do is reflect on the wisdom, "that's why they call it "fishing" and not "catching," and maybe start to think a little about how well we're going to do next time out.

I hedged my bet as best I could, preparing several flavors of cooked cornmeal bait (yellow meal with vanilla, white with anise, etc.) and inviting good friend Roland Hagon to join me in this expedition. Roland added his large metal washtub to our equipage — a tub which had seen hard service over the years holding our ocean catches of whiting, ling and mackerel. We somehow found room for the tub in my little eight-foot tin boat, "The Karp Katcher," which we double anchored across current in the channel of the Delaware River at Bull's Island State Park, Raven Rock, New Jersey.

For an uncomfortably long part of the morning, the carp taught me a proper lesson in humility.

"I sort of promised," I told Roland, who assumed a superior air and suggested that in the future, I make promises I knew I could keep. Just as I was framing a fitting response, the welcome sound of drag tearing off a spinning reel greeted my ears.

Carp are always wonderful, powerful fish, but nowhere do they generate the power and sheer excitement as much as in the deep, swift flowing channel of a big river. My carp more than lived up to his billing, fighting me every inch of the way to the boat, with powerful, surging runs against the tightening drag of my dependable Mitchell 300 reel.

I netted the fish and gingerly worked the #6 hook out of the carp's mouth and deposited him in the tub. Shortly thereafter, a second, slightly smaller carp hit Roland's cornmeal offering and after a spirited fight, followed my fish into the tub. Both fish were alive but on close inspection, it appeared that mine was somewhat the worse for wear. So we released it back into the river and immediately transported Roland's 9 pound fish back to the Somerville Inn.

The party was held and I can reliably report that both the book and the carp were instant hits. Hundreds of people, including members of the press, strolled by to view the carp in the bathtub even before viewing "The Carp in the Bathtub." I was thanked profusely by Barbara and Gene and introduced to a number of people as the fisherman who had caught the carp. I wanted to tell them that it was Roland's fish, honestly I did. (Well, at least I'm owning up to the truth now, twenty+ years after the fact!)

At party's end, true to the spirit and letter of her book, Barbara and her husband took the carp to nearby Peter's Brook in Somerville and gently released it. As it happens, Peter's Brook flows eventually into the main body of the Raritan River, a wonderful habitat for thousands of large carp. It was everything the two children in Barbara's story could have wished.

Perhaps a future reprint of Barbara's book will have a footnote about this ending. If so, I'll buy new copies for my grandchildren, whose mother has already told them some of the missing details.

CHAPTER 2

Varieties Of Carp

"COMMON CARP." Called this by most, although this beast is far from a "commoner" in my book, more like a Queen or King, but for now, let's just say that the most commonly found carp throughout the world is probably the common carp. Some call them "Scaled Carp." Generally speaking, American's refer to them as "German Carp," but some American's use far worse names. More on that next chapter!

"LEATHER CARP." This fish is totally scaleless, and has skin like leather, thus the name. Commonly found in Europe, a leather carp is built more round than a common carp, and grows to enormous size. Frankly, of the few thousand carp that I have caught throughout the states, I have never seen a leather, although I am told that, years ago, they were often found in fish stores that specialized in the sale of carp.

"MIRROR CARP." Many mirror carp are rounded like leather's, but the only ones that I have ever seen had the exact build of a German carp. Some mirror's are nearly full-scaled, with these scales being of uniform size and proportion.

Over the many years that I have fished for carp, the dozen or so mirror's that I have seen all had the same basic scale formation. A dozen scales here, maybe three there, twenty more over in this spot, etc. Some of the scales were as small as your pinky nail and others would have done a tarpon proud. Consistent was the fact that few scales were the same size and shape. One two inches high and sickle-shaped might be found alongside another

An 11 pound mirror with his friend,
Delaware River Park Ranger, Dave Bank.

that is nearly normal.

The truth be known, to an unsuspecting angler in Russia, a mirror might look like something that came out of the Chernobyl accident. In the United States, maybe something that was the result of a mother carp needing Thalidomide to help procreate. Looks goofy, like a mutant, but, if at the end of my line, a NICE fish!

"GRASS CARP." Grown to control weed growth, this fish is fine if kept where it belongs, in a controlled space, but sometimes they wander away, and serious problems have resulted. I spoke to Peter Aarrestad, Fisheries Biologist for the State of Connecticut and resident expert on grass carp. He told me that a "Grass Carp Symposium" was held in Gainesville, Florida in March of 1994, this fish being of such interest to people.

They are also called Triploid Grass Carp. In 1994, a specimen was killed in the main body of the Raritan River in New Jersey by some fool with a bow and arrow. It weighed nearly FORTY POUNDS. The fish should not have been there, but that is another story. Grass carp are intentionally stocked in fully enclosed ponds, with no outlet to other waters, as a means of reducing dense weed growth.

Rules differ but generally speaking, you cannot stock your own pond without permission from your state government, and the real reason for this is that government does not want these critters to go elsewhere.

I had been writing a fishing column for the *Somerset Messenger Gazette*, a newspaper that covered most of Somerset County, New Jersey back in the 70's, when Bill Roach (a name fit for an angler), head of the Somerset County Planning Board, called me with a "news tip." The result was that I took a ride to Montgomery, New Jersey, to a string of farm ponds run by a Chinese gentleman who was rearing grass carp (called "Amur" carp then), for sale to Chinese restaurants as customer food. I remember picking some grass from the shoreline of one of the ponds and throwing it into the water. Quiet and peaceful until then, the water burst with life and fish climbed all over each others backs to get at the food. The reason for being called "grass carp?" Trust me, I saw it happen. They eat grass!

"GOLDFISH." Yes, goldfish! They are indeed a member of the carp family, even though most that you have seen were a few inches long and contained in a circular bowl in your living room. Also called "Koi," perhaps a Japanese name, they are normally much rounder than common or grass carp, and they can reach several pounds in weight. In fact, I caught one back in the 50's at Prospect Park Lake, Brooklyn, N.Y. that weighed exactly 3½ pounds!

When kept in the open, in larger bodies of water, goldfish grow! Again, many are rounded, still others have the same shape as common carp, but are far different in color. No doubt many of you have been to parks where a dozen different shades of goldfish can be seen, all interwoven too. A fish may be part gold and part black. Still others, with white mixed in. In-bred so as to show unusual beauty, goldfish were and remain common in Asia.

A location that comes to mind is the Mystic, Connecticut Aquarium where some people are even more interested in watching the multi-colored carp swimming around than the far more difficult to keep in captivity seals that are nearby!

"JAPANESE CARP." Honestly, I do not remember ever reading about this particular fish anywhere, but I do recall catching quite a few in the Delaware River in New Jersey, and that is the name that I use for them. Truth be known, it really is a carp that is shaped like a rounded goldfish, but colored more like a German carp. Maybe a bit darker than a "common," and, like goldfish, without the "whiskers" of a common, I have caught at least one hundred of these fish and for lack of a book to look it up in, I will still feel that it can be called "Japanese."

CHAPTER 3

Names

"◄●□☆✱■○▶!" I suppose the most commonly used name for carp in America is something like: "!◄●□☆✱■○▶!," an exclamation, rather than a name, but still too often used. Most people who hook carp in America curse them with an expletive similar to the one shown above. Kind of dumb, but the numbers of carp lovers in the States are increasing daily. Everyone who breaks a line on one, or worse yet, smashes a rod, and perhaps worst of all, loses a favorite spinning outfit into the drink, is a carp lover waiting to happen. Eventually these folks will get religion and join with us carp addicts. Until then, let them cuss all they want, fools that they be!

"Queen of Rivers." Sir Izaak Walton referred to carp as "Queen of Rivers" and this truly is a wonderful name for so fine a beast.

"King of Fishes." This is what people used to call carp many years ago in Asia. Note the difference in sex between people from different lands describing the very same fish. Read on for an even sillier example of often incorrect sexual identification caused by a name.

"King." According to Dan Gapen, author of "Why Fish Carp," many English anglers refer to lunker carp as "King" and for good reason. They are the rulers of their waters!

"Mr. Man." This is the moniker that I hung on carp about thirty years ago and I really don't think that I stole the name from anyone else. The reason that I call EVERY carp "Mr. Man" is simple enough. In my opinion, they take a line and run with the speed, power and turning agility of a male Olympian. Over the years many readers have asked me, recalling the name that I have used, "When are you going to write a book about Mr. Man?" Well, here 'tis.

"Man." Another variety of the above name, my dear departed friend and fellow carp lover, Sam Krugler of Highland Park, N. J. and Boynton Beach, Florida, shortened my name and called a carp a "Man," after fishing with me for them several times. The funny thing about this is that I think that most very large carp are females and therefore, Sir Isaak was correct and the British, Asians and myself who call them a king or a man are usually wrong. Know what? They will always be "Mr. Man" to me!   .

"Puckermouth." More from Dan Gapen — kind of self-explanatory, really. Just look one in the face and after a while, it puckers. Also referred to as "Puckerpuss," for the same reason. No, I have never kissed one fully on the mouth, but I sure do love them!

"Ole' Buglemouth." Yet another name from author Gapen that allows you to close your eyes and draw a picture which describes a fish, carp do indeed have a mouth that could be used to call the troops to battle. I much prefer to think of that mouth surrounding my hook instead of kissing or making music, but then again, when I stick that steel home, it causes a combination of love for the fish, tied in with the music of a screaming drag. Hey, maybe these are more than nicknames!

"Big Scaler." Here is one of the best names you can use, because other than a naked leather carp, these overgrown members of the minnow family have enormous scales! My transplanted South Carolinian fishing buddy, Ron Bern (who you will hear from later), probably thinks that he created this name but even though he has released FOUR carp (damn him) bigger than anything I ever caught, I still think that it is a name that I created. They sure do have big scales though, don't they?

"Fish." Ron says that this name for sure is his creation, and he may be right. When either of us fishes without the other, and reports later on how many "fish" he caught, neither need to ask "what kind of fish?" Anything else has its proper name used, but a carp IS a fish, and needs no further description. You see, we really think that carp belong at the top of the list of FISH.

"Schpeagal carp." Here is one that not many have heard, but for some reason, mirror carp were called "Schpeagal" by some folks who came from Eastern Europe.

"Chicken carp." Yet one more name used for mirror carp, and not a very good one! No "chickens," these, they are carp that are built like common carp but have a weird scale formation. All were "Chicken" or "Schpeagal" to me until I sat down to write this book and found their true name to be "Mirror." I remember clearly my first one, it was while fishing from shore on the Wal-kill River in New York State. I thought that I had caught a freak of nature! Another one that comes to mind, with a smile on my face as I type, was the chicken that my dad caught with me in the Raritan River at Raritan, New Jersey. He was bad of foot, partially crippled, and had just begun his decline from cancer when the eight pounder took drag! Years poured off of him and dad became a teenager as he fought the fish to my waiting net.

"Double," or "Double Figure." Damn! I thought that this too was a name of my invention until I saw it used at length in several British magazines that were all or partially devoted to carp angling. What is a "double?" It is a carp that has reached at least ten pounds in weight.

"Twenty" or "Thirty." Iain Sorrell, fellow member of "The Carp Anglers Group," first told me about these names late in

1995, adding, the cur, that he had caught at least 20 carp over 20 pounds that year in the Connecticut River near where he lives. Self-explanatory, and attributable directly to Great Britain where carp that have reached weight equaling these numbers are referred to this way. If a carp weighs twenty five pounds, she still is a "Twenty," and the happy angler need only say he put another "Twenty" back. Everyone will know what that means.

Nigel Griffen holding a
39 pound common he caught in Mass.

CHAPTER 4

Killing
And Eating Carp

_____

_____

_____

_____

_____

_____

_____

_____

_____

End of Chapter[1]!

_____

---

[1] _This book is not about killing carp. I have not killed one in at least twenty years and do not intend to ever kill another one. This is not to be taken as a lecture, just as a simple statement of fact. Carp give me far too much pleasure to even dream about destroying one for any reason._

It is true that folks eat carp, and if you want to know about that, some carp books may tell you how to, shudder, clean and cook 'em, but friends, not my book!

CHAPTER 5

Connecticut

W ell known for its wonderful countryside, with many places to go to hide from life, Connecticut is home to some excellent angling too! Exposed to saltwater on its eastern side, the "Nutmeg" State also has lots and lots of super freshwater to fish in.

A fellow who seems to know far more about carp fishing in Connecticut than most is a former resident of England, Iain Sorrell, who we have talked about already in our dedication section. Iain told me that he caught over 20 carp in 1995 alone that hit or exceeded the 20 pound mark!

A transplant from the South of England, Iain introduced me to "The Carp Anglers Group," a countrywide organization, which I joined late in 1995. He also shared some secrets with me regarding bait, preparation, styles, etc.

Iain simply loves to fish along the shores of the Connecticut River. This very long body of water is home to more than carp alone. Shad migrate up its ranges, trout are aggressively stocked in it by the Department of Environmental Protection in the state, and I think that salmon may have already been introduced to the river. Striped bass? Yup, but who cares?! What Iain is after, and surely finds, is my old friend, "Big-Scaler!"

Mr. Sorrell fishes the whole year 'round at a Power Plant's hot water outlet, where the water temperature is generally near 80 degrees. This is plenty warm enough for carp, and whenever possible, he is out there doing his thing! The facility is located at Haddam, Connecticut, but the river gives up carp in normal warm water times all up and down its shoreline.

*Here is Iain with the 25 pound common he used
"Popped-up" feed corn to catch, 9/95.*

Yet one more Connecticut resident who is here from England, is
Nigel Griffen of Eurotackle, a company that specializes in the
sale of carp equipment, English style. Call him at 1-203-874-7107
and he will be glad to send you a catalog. Nigel is a member of the
Carp Anglers Group, which we have spoken about several times

already. What he is, more than anything else, is a super Carper!

Other areas to find carp here are Candlewood Lake at Danbury, and in particular, the Housatonic River, especially below the main dam at Kent Falls. There are several lakes that adjoin or are fed by the Housatonic that hold carp also.

If you have not learned enough about fishing for carp in Connecticut, I have given you the telephone numbers of Iain Sorrell and Nigel Griffen. Chances are they will not be home when you call, probably out doing some, harumph, "research" on carp angling, but they will get back to you.

I was touted onto Iain by a friend of his at the D.E.P., Bill Hyatt, who also told me how I could reach his co-worker, Peter Aarrestad, the true grass carp expert in Connecticut, and Peter supplied me with most of the material I used when talking to you in Chapter Two about the grass carp type of member of the carp clan.

I was happy to find out that carp caught in the Connecticut River, with their very long life span, are on the State's eating advisory list, which says what you should or should not eat, based on your own health condition. Connecticut tells people who are not in perfect health that these carp may be harmful to them if eaten in sufficient quantity. Prior contaminates in the river that may have been ingested by grandma or grandpa carp could get passed on to folks dining on a meal of "Mr. Man." Now isn't that simply great news? GOOD! People are warned to not eat carp caught in this river, and no doubt other than people who are really in need, know to release our good friends to fight another day!

———————

CHAPTER 6

New York

Home to many fine athletic teams, cultural attractions, the fabled "White Way" of Broadway, New York is also where dynamite carp angling goes on, even though many anglers have no clue that we "New Yawker's" even own any tackle.

"THE CITY"

Born and brought up in Brooklyn, my first carp was caught at Prospect Park Lake in the Borough. New York City consists of five boroughs and while it is a real "city," carp are still in at least four of the five boroughs of New York City. The Bronx is known for its Yankees and wonderful Zoo, but I am not certain if it holds any carp. The Borough of Queens on the other hand, has several lakes where you can find them. Generally the more rounded "Japanese carp," I remember catching them on pieces of salt-water bloodworms in a pond near the old World Fair Grounds. Alley Pond Park too comes to mind as a spot in Queens.

I just told you about Prospect Park Lake in Brooklyn. Well, Manhattan also has a big park, with a nice lake — Central Park Lake, which holds big-scaler's. Try to avoid night fishing at both of these lakes. It could ruin your whole day — and maybe, your life.

Last on the list of borough's is Staten Island, which tried to secede from the City in 1995, because its residents view their little skinny island as a state all to itself. As small as it is, Staten Island (also called Richmond) has many lakes, most of which contain carp. I fished a few of these ponds back in the 50's and

60's, but for more current details I turned to Pat, proprietor of Scag's Bait & Tackle, a store frequented by many area fresh-water enthusiasts.

I remembered Clove Lake and Pat said that while it holds some fish, it feeds Martling's and Brook's Ponds which house some huge beasts. The largest lake on the island is Silver Lake and Pat said he has seen several "Twentie's" swimming there, lighter in color than most carp. The former Proctor & Gamble Factory has a series of five ponds behind it and two of them contain many carp.

"LONG ISLAND"

If you get to the eastern end of Queens you will eventually get into Long Island, containing first Nassau, and then Suffolk Coun-ty. A wonderful place to fish for carp was Smith Pond, but I personally messed it up for out of towners. Calling in a catch of a 17 pounder by fellow fisherman Harold Weiss to friend Jim Hur-ley of a New York newspaper, for him alone to know, Jim's note somehow got into his fishing column and the next week, fifty anglers lined the previously empty shoreline. A fence containing signs saying "Resident's Only" ringed the lake only a week later. Funny how quick government can move sometimes. The lake is fed by Hempstead Lake which also has goodly numbers of carp. There are several other lakes on Long Island that hold carp but I don't want to tell you about them and get them closed up too.

THE HUDSON RIVER

A very underfished body of water, the Hudson has been going through a clean-up process for many a year. It previously was a dumping ground for every kind of contaminant known to man, and it still has a long way to go. The Hudson does hold carp, lots of them, and anglers who fish from shore, mostly above the George Washington Bridge, put together some respectable catches.

UPSTATE

A term that loosely describes a very long stretch of land, and so vast that we can merely touch on "Upstate" here. If you head far enough north, you will hit Lake Ontario and charter boat captain, Tom Schafer of Paladin Charters said that the Sodus Bay section produces big carp each summer. Lake Ontario is enormous and also needs its own book, so let me just say simply that carp addicts catch carp there!

I made a call before Christmas of '95 to the New York State Department of Conservation in Albany and found a wonderful lady named Marge who sent me a copy of "Carp in North America," and was then good enough to connect me to a carp enthusiast, her co-worker, Doug Stang.

Doug reported that the Tomhannck Reservoir, located northeast of Albany, has a huge population of carp. Situated in Rensallear County, a permit is needed from the City of Troy to fish here. Doug said that the New York State record carp was taken there in 1995, weighing 50.4 pounds. The prior record, 41.2, came from the same lake! He added that in the central part of the state, carp are at Seneca Lake. Ditto in the Susquehanna River, from Binghamton down to where it joins the Hudson.

A Roundout Creek "double" caught way back when the author had hair — WAY BACK WHEN!

The St. Lawrence River contains carp galore. Another fine place is Roundout Creek. That brings me to the place that I told you about way at the start: the Walkill River.

THE WALKILL RIVER

Like the Millstone River in Central New Jersey, this river runs backwards! Tracking from south to north, against gravity, I have fished it from Newburgh up to Walden, then to Modena & Gardiner, continuing to New Paltz and Rifton, catching carp in every spot. Most of this goes back to the 50's through the 70's, but the river remains as it was. Maybe a shot or two from pollution messed it

Manny with a 14½ pounder caught in the 50's in the Walkill River.

up, but the Walkill is a fine river today for carp lovers.

In 1993 I fished at the exact spot outside of New Paltz that I had last fished maybe thirty years before, and caught a "double" on four kernels of canned corn, with a little ultra-lite rig and four pound mono. It was, of course, released, and I drove away thirty years younger.

My favorite story about The Walkill, other than the one about friend Maurice in the Foreword, involved another carp that got away to tell the story.

I fished a great deal with my cousins Ted and Russ as a boy and then as a young man. We spent a weekend once up at Gardiner and it was nearing the end of the trail.

Russ and I had each landed at least one carp, but Ted, older and wiser than we, just had not gotten the net under one yet and we were to head home in an hour or so. Realizing he was getting cranky, I moved away, far away, downstream.

Minutes later I heard Russ scream and watched him wave wildly in my direction. Then rather fleet of foot, I ran over and found Ted standing, with rod held high, the solid glass stick bent half-way over, and a silly grin was spread from ear to ear.

Our goal, Russ's and mine, was to make sure Ted caught his carp. It was Ted's car, mind you. The fight wore on, but the shoreline was clear and dry, with plenty of room to chase the fish up and downstream. The carp swam way out, and after a while, Ted's grin turned to a frown because the carp hung him up, way, way offshore.

I tell you about a carp that I had to walk out after in my New Jersey chapter. Well, here, Russ and I helped dress Ted up in chest high waders and off he walked!

Walking and reeling, in perfect time, Ted gave no slack as he got further out into the river. It was not deep, and the current was modest, two good things indeed. He felt that the fish was still on, but snagged under some sunken wood.

Ted must have gone two hundred feet from land and then the water began to lap in over the top of his waders, but he still walked. In only a few more feet, he kicked into a little branch and then found more wood parallel to the bottom. Following his line, Ted actually found the fish behind a nearby piece of wood and made an arc, a looong arc, with his boot around its body.

Yelling to us that he reached the fish, the very, very big fish, he kicked gently at the wood and finally broke it up and the fish swam out, free of the snag, and still on the hook. Unencumbered by obstacles and filled with strength anew, the beast did a beastly thing, as Ted held the rod high above the water, trying to back up and avoid drowning. The carp took a sudden and nasty lurch downstream, and GOT OFF!

Mind you, this was forty or more years ago, and Ted was way out, but my eyesight was better too than today. Without further word, Russ and I watched him rear back with the rod, as if he were Captain Ahab holding a spear, and then Ted launched the glass into the drink, far away. Had Ted been a member of our Olympic Team then, he could have won the javelin toss by ten yards.

No additional words were exchanged in the car as we headed home for quite a while!

CHAPTER 7

New Jersey

My being a resident of New Jersey since 1964, you will find more in "Gone Fishin' for Carp" about "Ole' Buglemouth" in this state than elsewhere, but that is only because most of my fishing for them since then has been in our "Garden State."

This book contains a separate sub-chapter about The Delaware River, because it is so wonderful a place to fish for carp, so if you see little reference here to "The Big D," have no fear, it just deserves separate space.

DELAWARE TRIBUTARIES

The Delaware has many tributaries that feed it so let's talk a bit about them here. In Mantua, I spoke to Larry, owner of

*Twenty-eight pound German that Tim Swift fished
out of a Delaware tributary in South Jersey.*

Larry's Fisherman's Cove, a Bait & Tackle Store, and he told me that Mantua Creek gives up lots of big carp every spring. He added that Woodbury Creek in West Deptford Township is yet another feeder that carp charge up to feed and spawn in.

There really are quite a few other creeks and streams that are hooked up to the Delaware. Another that comes to mind which produces fine carp catches in is Rancocas Creek, which runs all the way from Delanco and Riverside way to the west, past Rancocas Woods, & turns into a trickle further eastward. It then opens up again, continuing on to or beyond Browns Mills, not far from McGuire Air Force Base, many, many more miles to the east by southeast.

DELAWARE & RARITAN CANAL

Yet one more skinny body of water that carp can be found in is called The Delaware & Raritan Canal. Built for inland transportation of barges via a series of lift locks, the canal begins at Bull's Island State Park in Raven Rock, N.J. on the Delaware. It sneaks in and out all the way to its ultimate connection, way to the east by northeast, at New Brunswick, where it hooks up to the Raritan River.

Barges drawn by mules walking along a towpath used to bring materials eastward this way years ago. The canal is of such historic importance that State Senator Raymond Bateman authored legislation creating The Delaware & Raritan Canal State Park, and added the canal itself to our list of historic sites.

All that to the side, you know what? The canal has carp swimming in its entire length, and I have caught many fine specimens in it, from one end to the other.

I remember one particularly silly experience while fishing for trout. Dummy that I was, I left a rod down alongside of me at a little overpass below the Stockton Lock, baited with corn kernel for trout. I did have, I swear, the drag open in the event of a lunge from the expected trout, but a fish with far more muscle took! The rod was launched skyward and into the drink! Picking up another outfit, I cast downstream a bit and luck have it, got into

*The D&R Canal gave up this 8 pounder to
Carp Anglers Group's George Harsel.*

the line right away. I retrieved the rod, tightened the drag, and caught the fish! Released of course, it swam off, and probably tells the story to this day to its grandchildren about the rod that got away!

THE RARITAN RIVER
NORTH AND SOUTH BRANCHES

Here's one for the books! There are two branches of the Raritan that eventually join at Branchburg (maybe the reason for the town's name)? I found out from Lisa Barnow of N.J. Fish, Game & Wildlife that the north branch of the Raritan starts at Mend-

New Jersey State Record carp as of 1995 —
Billy Friedman's 47 pounder, South Branch!

ham Township, and the south branch of the river begins at Budd Lake. What's wrong with this picture? Budd Lake is well to the NORTHwest of Mendham Township, so the South Branch begins in a more northerly locale than the North Branch. Listen, take two aspirin for your headache, and read on.

Each branch contains many carp, along with trout, bass, etc. The State Record for carp was broken in 1995 by a young man named Billy Friedman who landed a mirror carp ON MY SIX-TIETH BIRTHDAY, 8/29, at the South Branch. The prior record came from The Delaware River. Now listen, Billy, don't you think it would have been nice to credit ME with the record as a birthday present? No? Well, I tried anyway.

THE MAIN BODY

Once the river connects up at Branchburg, it travels downstream only a mile or two to Duke (Doris Duke) Island State Park, and runs eastward quite a long way, going down several waterfalls, and the outlet of the Delaware & Raritan Canal appears just before New Brunswick. The river is quite wide here and continues down, hooking up with the South River, and finally empties out into Raritan Bay and then into the Atlantic. Somewhere around South River, it becomes brackish, but the South River itself also holds carp.

I have released several hundred carp back into the main body, in a stretch that runs only ten miles or so, from just above Duke Island Park, down to the town of Raritan itself. In the chapter devoted to names of carp I told you about the "chicken" (mirror) carp my dad caught. Two other events stand out above all others that took place in the Raritan.

One was a half-mile below the confluence of the two branches at Branchburg, fishing from shore with good buddy Ron Bern. I hooked a "double-figure," for sure, and the critter hung me up in overhanging tree branches. Ron helped me get into a set of waders as I held the rod, and I pushed off into the water. Reeling and walking, I reached the tangle, got it loose, and off the fish went, mid-river, as I backed up to shore. The fight continued until the big beauty was released. I have a far funnier but still similar story for you, with an unhappy ending, in the New York section — Walkill River part.

Next story is one you might not want to tell your kids. I was fishing below what is called "Headgates" at Duke Island Park with Lenny Kraus. I had six carp and he had caught dork (you only forget when the other guy beats you), when I heard lots of noise upstream. Looking up above the "gate" I saw a gaggle of canoes and youngsters, along with a rubber raft and two "grownups." Obviously they saw us fishing and would go around us ("portage") to continue downstream. Well, NOT! The two men came ashore ten yards from us, and the kids put their dozen canoes and rubber boat in, just dead in front of us, from 50 to 100 feet out! I yelled at the kids and their leaders, to no avail, and was, to say the least, furious.

At that time we used to fish with a number four treble hook with wire around its perimeter, a device that held cooked corn meal balls (a/k/a "boilie's" or "Mommah-liggah") on very well. The kids were playing splashy-splashy, scaring the carp far away, when I gave up fishing for carp. I took the bait off of the treble hook that was rigged with a somewhat stiff rod and began to fish for rafts. One cast followed, perfectly placed. The egg sinker carried my hook to the offshore side of the empty raft, and I did it just perfectly! Two barbs were nicely stuck in the rubber and I reeled it to shore. With shaking hands I tore like an idiot at the raft until it became nothing but bits and pieces.

The two leaders, knowing this man was quite off his rocker, headed out to the kids with their canoe, prevailed upon the boys to board the remaining canoes, and off they went. I did catch one more carp before quitting and it fought much better than the raft!

THE MILLSTONE RIVER

Another excellent hunk of water that connects to the Raritan! This strange river runs from south to north, clearly against gravity, like the Walkill River in New York. It begins at Carnegie Lake in Kingston, not far from Princeton (wonder why we don't have a Queenston or Princesston?) The Millstone connects with the Raritan River at Manville.

Nearly destroyed by a pollution spill back in the 70's, the river has come back and holds thousands of carp once more. Approximately 100,000 fish, at least half of which being carp, were found floating belly up back around 1974. Again though, they are back!

This river offers many miles of shoreline to fish from along either side and while much is private land, there are many, many places to stand and enjoy the peace and quiet, disturbed only by the song of a bird, or the scream of a drag. A great place to take young people because the current is not strong and kids won't tire quickly here.

*Fourteen year old Justin Lerner caught these at
New Providence on the Passaic — note tails!*

THE PASSAIC RIVER

Starting up a bit to the north, my map tells me that the
Passaic River too empties into the Raritan! The Passaic is a bit
more polluted than some other rivers, but carp still manage to
survive and thrive in it. Much of this river travels past bigger
cities, and offers super shoreline space for folks who like to sit on
a bucket and wait 'em out.

OTHER PLACES

There are quite a few other rivers in Jersey to find carp in, but
I did not want to write a book about carp fishing IN New Jersey,
only to write a chapter about it.

We do have many lakes and ponds to fish for carp from also.
Lake Hopatcong in Morris County, the biggest lake in New Jersey, holds them, and so too does Round Valley Reservoir in Hun-

terdon County, I am told. My favorite though is Spruce Run Reservoir, also Hunterdon, chock-filled with carp that tear up the water with abandon, breaking rods, snapping line, and in general, scaring bass fishermen half-to-death by their splashing around.

Columbia Lake in Warren County holds carp, I was told by Bob Papson of Fish, Game & Wildlife, along with Paulinskill Lake and Paulinskill River in Sussex County. I caught quite a few at Paulinskill Lake some years back. Branchbrook Park Lake, at the outskirts of Newark, real "city" area, has a bunch of "puckerpuss'" too.

Carnegie Lake, where the Millstone starts, holds carp, and Maggot Michael of Manchester gave a display there to a friend of mine some time ago. He was going to give me a similar display too at Spruce Run Reservoir until I told him that his chum — Maggot Launcher, a slingshot, was illegal to use in our fair state, because some think of it as a weapon! You will hear more about Maggot Michael in the section about England.

CHAPTER 8

The Delaware River

The Delaware River is, in my opinion, the finest stretch of freshwater in our entire country. Home to countless trout in its upper branches — with shad, muskellunge, walleye, smallmouth bass, striped bass, and channel catfish below, a fine river indeed. There are many of us though who love "The Big D" for another fish, CARP, and it is loaded with them, for many a mile.

This book is not about The Delaware alone, or how it got its name. Since the book is about carp fishing and this river holds so many, we owe separate space to this excellent place. It may be our second longest river in America, with the Mississippi probably traveling a longer route.

At least two authors have written books devoted completely to The Delaware, and while neither is a carp addict, they do tell you much about it. I recommend highly the books put out by friends Joe Kasper and John Punola.

Starting way up north, Delaware River National Park Service Ranger Dave Bank told me that the river's west branch starts at Popacton Reservoir and its east branch begins at Cannonsville Reservoir. Both are in New York, and wonderful trout fishing can be had in each branch, along with shad.

While the branches may hold carp, more are found from the point that they join into one body of water, at Buckingham, Pa. on the west, and Hancock, N.Y. on the east side.

There are lots of boat ramps on either side of the river, and details can be found in Joe & John's books. I will give you a few locations, but they do a more complete job. Ditto where you can

*A true expression of feelings by 'Drew Bank (Dave's brother)
for his 14 pound catch!*

set up your five gallon bucket or fancy carp chair to sit on and wait 'em out. A few sites from me, but more from these two experts in their books.

Dave Bank just started to fish for carp in 1994, after being urged on by yours truly, and is already "hooked" big time! He knows the upper reaches of the river quite well already, being a ranger, and is a person who has caught loads of smallmouth and striped bass, plus shad, muskie and walleye. He said that a good

Snapper Pool is where Greg Price caught this 16 pound common.

area for carp can be found after launching his boat on the Pennsylvania side of the river at Smithfield. He heads upstream and fishes between Bushkill and Smithfield at Snapper Pool. Below a bit, but still above the launch site, is Poxono Pool, and he caught quite a few at both pools in 1995.

Dave also said that carp are found about four miles above the Delaware Water Gap, with a launch at Worthington State Park on the Jersey side. Once you head south to just below The Gap itself, you will find Old Mine Road on the Jersey side too. This is where the ranger office is, and a nice ramp is here, along with shore access for chair or pail. There are loads of carp nearby, including at what is called Arrow Island.

Dave asked me to tell you that the Park Service carefully monitors speed here, and actually uses radar guns to check lunatics out. Laws change, so I will not tell you anything other than you must learn and obey the law, in particular when the water is warmer and speed limits are reduced to protect those who canoe, kayak, or simply float downstream in old truck tire-tubes.

As you head below "The Gap," you reach Frenchtown on the east and there are several spots to fish from at shore's edge. The Pennsylvania side continues down to Point Pleasant where you can rent canoes, tubes, etc., but some folks fish from shore there too. Both sides have at least one ramp or two over the ten mile stretch from The Gap south.

We reach Byram on the Jersey side, just above Bull's Island State Park at Raven Rock, where the Delaware & Raritan Canal begins its long trip to the Raritan River. A good ramp is between Byram and the canal, and there is an area where you can launch from too in the park itself. Many people camp in the park, with anywhere from tents to fancy rigs in use. Our British and other camper friends may really like this area, because it offers some additional attractions beyond just a place to fish from.

There is a ramp across from Byram in Pennsylvania, and again, shore sitting room.

I have caught hundreds of carp, maybe more like one thousand of them, in the five miles stretch that runs from Byram to the Raven Rock Wing Dam. Common carp, mostly, but a few "chicken carp" (mirror), along with gold carp and what I described to you already as Japanese carp, a bit darker than a "common," but with the rounded shape of a goldie.

Below Raven Rock is Stockton and Lambertville on my side of the river, and across to the west in Pennsylvania, we find New Hope. These three towns are wonderful tourist attractions, with fine restaurants, hotels, "Bed & Breakfast's," and fun shopping. For many though, they are merely great places to fish from. There are at least two more boat ramps in and around Lambertville, and I think that New Hope may have one. Again, shore fishermen can cast out, sit, and wait here. A huge Wing Dam is below Lambertville, and I have taken carp from it, as well as a bit downstream at Firemen's Eddy, where a small car-topper can be launched, and a dozen or two fishermen can sit. My father's last carp was caught while sitting on a beach chair at Firemen's Eddy. I remember every second of the entire experience, even though it was in 1973, from baiting to casting to helping him land and release the fish. He smiled, and for the moment, his cancer was gone.

Again, this river is extremely long and it eventually starts to receive saltwater a bit below Lambertville, from way to the south. Even though carp are not known for liking brackish water, there are at least twenty or thirty miles of water that receives brine on incoming tides below Firemen's Eddy, and carp are in all of them!

"The Big D," home of "MR. MAN!"

CHAPTER 9

Pennsylvania

Home of some huge landlocked striped bass, northern pike, tiger muskie and true muskellunge, there are a select few fishermen in Pennsylvania who also go after carp. This state is one of many that houses untold numbers of carp that get little or no attention at all!

Edwin Cooper, editor of "Carp in North America," and also "Fishes of Pennsylvania," was one person who helped me get information regarding the whereabouts of carp in his state. Rayestown Dam is a place that holds many. Famous for so-called "Game-fish" like striped and smallmouth bass, it also houses enormous carp. Kinzua Reservoir is another fine lake, located near the town of Warren, on the Upper Allegheny River.

Many of the large rivers in Pennsylvania contain carp. Bob Lorantas and Marty Marcinko work for the Division of Warmwater Species in the state, and shared some more details with me. Marty told me, (and he worked with the committee that produced the book, "Carp in North America") that the Lower Allegheny River, along with the Monongahela, Susquehanna, Juniata and Schuykill Rivers all have swarms of "Big-Scalers." I fished for carp along the banks of the Susquehanna, outside of Lancaster, Pa., one day, and caught several nice carp, without having a clue as to if the location had any fish at all, carp, or otherwise.

Bob and Marty said that Sayers Dam Lake in Bald Eagle State Park is home to carp, as well as Bald Eagle Creek itself. This is in Center County.

Perhaps the most interesting and unique place to find carp is in Hershey, Pa., where the street lights are shaped like Hershey Kisses, and the whole town smells like something you want to eat. Named for the chocolate folks, you can enjoy a pleasant day touring the factory, getting free samples, and going through Hershey Park. Chances are you will gain some weight just inhaling as you walk around, ingesting calories galore from the air alone. What I enjoyed doing too though was standing on a bridge in Hershey Park with people far younger than I. We were all feeding bread to carp, BIIIIG carp, and they rolled and splashed every time one of us would throw some bread into the water. Now this is a place that clearly has monster sized carp, but maybe not too good a place to fish in. Some spoil sport would probably say that it is illegal. Still nice to watch though.

The Delaware River runs past the eastern side of Pennsylvania, but I did not want to include it in this section. The Delaware was entitled to its own chapter, because it may be the best place to catch carp in throughout the entire world! Hopefully you enjoyed reading about "The Big D" before you got to this chapter.

CHAPTER 10

South Carolina
By Ronald L. Bern

The Southeastern United States is perfectly hospitable to carp. Clean, slow flowing rivers, massive lakes and abundant weed growth provide the venue and the menu actively prescribed for cyprinus carpio's development and growth — often to startling proportions. Curiously, however, even in rural regions where bottom fishing for catfish is a major preoccupation, carp fishing has historically inspired little excitement except in the hearts of the knowledgeable and the initiated.

One such was this writer, who more than 50 years ago learned to appreciate the fighting properties of carp during a rite of passage for South Carolinians known as "goin' to Santee Cooper." The Santee Cooper river basin is the watershed for a massive central strip of the state which includes people of 147 cities and towns. Virtually all of the state's interior rivers — the final being the Santee and the Cooper — contribute nutrients and riverine populations to the massive Lake Moultrie and thence south and east to the sea.

When informed by my father that a trip to Santee Cooper was imminent, visions of 60 lb. blue cat's crowded out such mundane concepts as arithmetic, spelling and household chores. Significantly, no fish even entered into the equation other than the massive catfish known to thrive in Lake Moultrie and in the Santee and Cooper Rivers.

Our tackle was precisely suited to our quarry: short steel rods, sturdy level wind reels and 50 lb. nylon line. Our bait was similarly specialized: cut chunks of mullet and even less savory rancid chicken intestines.

We camped out on the lake and applied ourselves in the most single-minded fashion, but the catfish were otherwise disposed. Neither large "bluecats" nor small were attracted to our offerings. An eight pound striped bass — part of the first experiments in America in stocking this saltwater fish in fresh waters — took my cut bait and provided virtually all of the excitement — and most of the protein — of an otherwise deathly quiet first day.

The second day was no better until late afternoon, when a certain Mr. Boggs — the elder statesman in our party of five — rummaged in his gear for what looked like a "pone" of corn bread. I watched with interest as he carefully carved off the outer crust, dampened a bit of the dry bread with water and began to knead it with bits of cotton. When he had worked the cotton thoroughly through the dampened corn mixture, he retrieved his weighted line, threw away the mullet, and buried his hook in the cotton-threaded mixture.

"Goin' carp fishing," Mr. Boggs said. "That cotton'll keep the bait on the hook."

I kept one eye on my rod and the other on Mr. Boggs, whose 70 summers had been divided roughly equally between cotton farming and creek fishing. He cast far out into the lake's calm surface, carefully opened the "brakes" on his old Shakespeare level wind reel and set the outfit down in a forked stick. Then he sat back, extracted his bag of Bull Durham tobacco and rolled a smoke. In almost no time at all, his rod suddenly lunged up out of the fork and raced toward the water. Mr. Boggs managed to grab it as the first eye of the rod entered the water. He set the hook and thereupon began a wonderful struggle between a powerful fish and a skilled fisherman. The stout line undoubtedly made the difference between success and failure and when the big German carp finally came to net, I felt an extraordinary excitement just looking at his coppery heaving sides.

"Could I.?" I started to ask, but Mr. Boggs was way ahead of me.

"Get your rod. Let's get it baited," he said. He released his fish unharmed and began carving pieces from his cornmeal pone.

As I cast the baited hook, I wanted nothing more in the world than to catch a carp. To this day, that fishing sentiment remains consistent. (To my continuing surprise, it is shared by few. There is vast enthusiasm in my adopted state of New Jersey for trout — not wily, native brookies or browns in pristine mountain streams, but nine and ten inch stocked fish, often only hours out of hatcheries. Yet the appetite for powerful, exciting tackle busting carp is almost nowhere in evidence. Strange!).

Mr. Boggs caught another, smaller carp, then a larger one, then one larger still. Silently I prayed a small boys prayer for just one chance.

When my first carp finally hit, I was holding the rod in my hands and the sensation was not unlike a charge of electricity up both arms. I managed to set the hook and in a state approaching delirium, I gained line and gave line, ranged up and down the bank and finally waded to my knees in water — all to the whoops of encouragement from my older and more experienced companions. It was a lovely fight, a fight that travels with me in memory undiminished down all these years. The carp, which weighed about eight pounds, finally came to the net and was released.

But with all the pleasure the Lake Moultrie carp gave us that trip, when we returned to Santee Cooper two years later, it was with catfish again in mind and no thought of carp at all. In fact, it was not until I moved to New Jersey 20 years later and met my fishing partner Manny Luftglass that I discovered another unappeasable appetite for carp fishing; indeed, one that surpassed even my own, as did his skill. With that meeting began a lifetime of pleasure on the lakes and rivers of the Garden State, more often than not, in quest of carp.

Significantly, we fish for carp not because of a failure of other opportunities. Indeed, we are surrounded by fine impoundments loaded with trophy sized hybrid bass, lake trout, brown trout, largemouth and smallmouth bass, pike and pickerel — all of which come to our nets in more than satisfying sizes and quantities. But none save the largest of the hybrid bass approximate the fight of even a modest sized carp.

The lack of interest among others continues to surpass our understanding. Occasionally it is especially well illustrated. For example, two eel fishermen working the channel of the Delaware River watched us in one titanic battle after another with big river carp one summer afternoon, even as they hooked and deposited a few small slimy eels in a bucket. On the way to the dock, one asked what we were fishing for and we replied "carp." The other asked us, in all seriousness: "How come you want to catch those trash fish?"

Surely, though, no such attitude persists in my home regions in the deep south, I assumed. But a recent telephone conversation with Mr. Val Nash of the South Carolina Department of Natural Resources disabused me of that notion.

"Subsistence fishermen keep carp, although they don't brag about it," he told me. "We don't get reliable reports from creel counts in the field because most fishermen won't even admit to catching carp."

Well, frankly, that is fine with me. I am pleased that visions of channel cats and undersized stocked rainbows dance in the heads of fishermen there and here.

For me, the dream is a powerful strike, a shrieking drag and a hard fought, twenty minute scrap with a lunging river carp, whether it be the legendary Santee of my childhood or the mighty Delaware.

Here's Ron with a nice carp he caught many years later in "New Joisey."

CHAPTER 11

Other States

Telling you about the four states that I know best should not be taken as trying to say that these are the best among the fifty — they are merely those that I know more about. Ron Bern, transplanted here in "Joisey" from South Carolina, has shared some of his knowledge about that state with you.

As to other carp homes, maybe the most impressive carp sighting I ever made was at Lake Mead at the joint of Arizona and Nevada. We were a group of motor homes out traveling through some western states late in the 80's, and I broke away from camp to sneak out for an hour or two.

I found a very large marina and walked out to its end, finding youngsters there who had bought fish pellets from a coin operated device, similar to a gumball machine. The kids were throwing the pellets into the water and it boiled with hundreds of swarming carp, anywhere from a few pounds up to thirty and forty pounders! Popcorn too was chased around and sucked in by these beasts.

The time was right and the place was at hand. I walked away, maybe one hundred yards, to where no one was present, and I put together the ultra-lite rod I had been carefully hiding. Opening the can of corn that was in my pocket, I stuck a few kernels on the number eight Eagle Claw bait holder hook and dropped it down right where I was standing. I could see carp straight down at bottom, about 15 feet away in the clear water. Not a tap, smell, or look followed.

I took the four pound line up, put the rod down, and chummed a few kernels. Immediately, the fish ate. I tried the rod again and, NOTHING. More chum, and more eating took place.

One evening at Guantanamo Bay, Cuba, while wearing Navy clothing, I did the same thing with shrimp. Little barracuda ate, but not from my hook with rod in hand. I put the rod down and hand-threw the shrimp baited hook and caught five barracuda before they got smart.

This time, I put the green rod down on the dock, baited the hook again, placed a bunch of kernels AND the baited hook in the palm of my hand, and dropped it all in. Several carp swam up, taking in the freebies AND one took my hook. I caught and released four common carp from four to eleven pounds in an hour that way before the rest of the crew got wise.

BOOKS

If you really want to know more about other states in America that hold carp, check out the two books already discussed, Dan Gapen's great "Why Fish Carp?" and "Carp in North America," put out by the American Fisheries Society.

Gapen is a real expert, based in Minnesota, and his book will tell you how carp fishing styles change from area to area. He also has pictures of some pretty ladies holding some also pretty carp.

"Carp in North America" tells about record fish by state and shares knowledge of a list of over 100 carp waters located in another thirty or forty states and provinces of Canada. It talks too about tournament sites, etc.

CARP ANGLERS GROUP

I saved what could be the best for last in our search for the hiding places of carp in the United States. As 1995 was coming to its end, I received my membership card in the non-profit organization, "Carp Anglers Group," as recommended to me by Iain Sorrell, the Connecticut Yankee by way of the South of England I told you about before.

My membership packet contained wonderful reading material, which has helped me prepare this book. In the packet too were details for how to buy the wild and crazy stuff that Englishmen have grown to know and love as superior carp catching equipment. From a "where to" standpoint, just in their November/ December newsletter alone, I found out about a fantastic encounter with a zillion carp on the Chicago River in Illinois, + fishing for them in Minnesota, New York, and California. Senior members of the board are in Kansas, Illinois, Michigan and Connecticut, and members are located in most states, plus Canada and England.

To get an application for membership if you are interested in joining, write to:

The Carp Anglers Group
Box 69
Groveland, IL 61535

The fee is $20, well worth the money!

Where else to find carp in North America? Darn near everywhere. The problem is not finding carp, it is in finding carp lovers!

CHAPTER 12

England

The danger in writing a book on a subject that you know you are an expert in is that, oftentimes, you find out how very little you know. Once upon a time, before I started to do the research for "Gone Fishin' for Carp," I was convinced that there was little I did not know. Silly me!

The basic difference between fishing for carp in England and America is that so much respect is paid to the sport in Great Britain, and so little occurs here.

The photo's that I have seen of carp caught in England all have the exact same appearance. Generally, a fat fish, held sideways, over a blanket of sorts, cradled lovingly in the arms of a smiling angler. As a fishing writer for several newspapers in New Jersey, most of the pictures that I have seen of carp caught hereabouts were of dead or dying carp!

A growing number of American's have realized that carp are what they are, glorious fish to be enjoyed, and released alive. Sad to say, some of the pictures in this book are of carp being held under their gills, fish that probably died from this rough handling, or even of already killed carp. Some American's even destroy carp for the sake of killing them, with bow and arrow, and then throw the dead fish away.

My experience in fishing in England consists of one single day, and none of the critters had big scales at all. I boarded a headboat at Brighton on which a dozen or two folks, mostly strangers to each other, paid their fares and took a chance at catching some fish. I remember clearly taking a half-dozen mackerel and perhaps fifteen plaice (a member of the flounder family.) Not hardly carp at all. Hopefully, to research a second printing one day, I might have to take a field trip to England for some, harumph, first hand reporting.

In America, all you need is a fishing license, a can of corn, and desire to catch carp. In England, it is altogether a different story! Much of the fishing in England is in still water, a lake or pond, and these facilities are generally private. The owner of the facility charges a fee for fishing, commonly called a "Day Ticket."

You may join a Syndicate or Club, which has very limited membership, and this entitles you to fish a Venue where no other anglers are allowed.

Now this fishing is not a couple of hours while sitting on a five-gallon bucket, friends. It is an adventure involving twenty-four straight hours OR MORE! While there is also river and stream fishing in England, again, most is done from non-moving water. Another major difference to me is that 90% of the carp that I have caught in the past twenty years have been from my boat, and nearly all carp angling in England is done from shore.

To put the material together for this chapter I turned to the four newspaper/magazines that I told you about in the dedication section, and then called Iain Sorrell, the fellow in Connecticut who came over here from England to practice his well-learned style of angling. Much of Iain's help came in the form of TRANS-LATING.

As discussed in the dedication section, I also met in person with Tony Broomer who cleared up many questions that remained in my mind regarding what some terms meant in AMERI-CAN! Tony belongs to a twelve person syndicate that has rights to fish a small pond in Bedfordshire which contains many very large mirror carp, and only four members fish very often.

If you are reading these pearls of wisdom in Great Britain, you certainly need no one to tell you what some of these terms mean, but if you are "Born in the U.S.A.," you would definitely get a major headache trying to figure them out, had Iain not helped me. Therefore before anything else, again, a tip of a Carper's hat to Iain. Next came Tony Broomer, here in New Jersey from Eng-

Pretty fully scaled mirror caught at Tony's favorite venue.

land, to further critique all. Hopefully, between both of them, they helped me know how to explain everything to you.

Many words are the same from one side of the pond to the other, but for those that I did not understand, I will use English terms and then put American lingo in parenthesis to explain their meaning to my countrymen. If this confuses you, my apologies, but honestly, what American knows what a, for example, HAIR RIG is? Sounds like something that Rapunzle might have used to contain her flowing locks in before throwing them down from the castle tower!

PREPARATION

When I am planning for a long fishing trip, maybe 100 miles out to sea for codfish on a thirty hour adventure, I take a lot of time getting ready, with all kinds of extra equipment, clothing, sleeping paraphernalia, etc. I have three or four rods, dozens of extra hooks, sinkers, lures, and so on. Food? For sure. Brit's plan for a carp trip in the same manner. We just aren't used to such a thing here.

Englishmen set out to go "Carping" at some rented space, on a Venue (piece of water), going to a Swim (exact spot), and maybe at a numbered Peg (this is done generally during a match and anglers draw raffles to see who gets which Peg). They fish a Margin (close to shore), or out further.

Folks from the U.K. carry a supply of equipment that might need a pack mule to haul. Remember now, this is no brief few hour shot at a local pond, it is a big deal! They have a Bivvy (domed tent) to sleep in, a sleeping bag, maybe a sleeping chair (padded for comfort, of course), perhaps another straight-backed padded chair to sit in during the daytime. Also several Torches (flashlights) for illumination, one or two camera's with extra film, a net big enough to land Moby Dick in, and an unhooking mat (honest, no translation needed, but they have soft mats to rest the carp in so as to not harm them!) The English have weigh bars, slings and sacks, all contraptions to contain carp in, for weighing and ultimate live release.

CLOSE SEASON

American's call the time that they cannot fish a spot, or for a variety of fish, the "Closed Season," so that pretty much explains the meaning, much the same, just that we add a "D" to "Close" in the States. "Close Season" was a time in England when much of their freshwater could not be fished, between 3/15 and 6/15 yearly. Much of that water was lakes, etc., but some moving water was also involved. Actually, all water containing "Coarse Fish" (Nearly all critters besides trout and salmon) were involved. The purpose was to close a venue to fishing so that fish could spawn, and in general, to "rest the waters."

A huge argument exists in England today among more devoted Carpers. Many stick to keeping away during the old Close Season days, other than to pre-bait (chum) or observe the water, even though most waters are no longer so restricted. A particularly enormous carp was caught in 1995 during these three months, one that contained at least ten pounds of roe. The same fish was again caught after 6/15 and it died from stress. While it was recognized, I believe, as the new English record carp, at first, many purists refused to acknowledge the catch.

RODS & REELS

Picture a cross between an ocean surf spinning outfit, a Lake Ontario extra long bait casting stick, and the steelhead rods that have grown in popularity throughout America. Take them all together, add features from each, along with a very high price tag, and you have a 12 foot long or so stick that could beat a horse. Match the rod to a very smooth-running spinning reel that holds a million feet of 10 pound test mono and that's the deal. Now go buy two or three more similar outfits and you are getting ready. By the way, every picture I saw of fishing in England involved folks using several of the exact same rods and reels. If any of them ever saw me in action, with a brown ultra-lite here, and an old Fenwick medium weight there, I think they would not want to fish near me.

Some of our English friends also have an extremely long Pole (an expensive one piece glass stick, an improvement over the old "cane pole" style used to this day here by worm dunkers). This Pole comes in handy for guys who want to actually reach out to put a Paste (dough bait) in front of carp at a Margin (close-to-shore honey-hole) without making a single sound.

SERIOUS STUFF

Two to three rods are rested parallel to shore on a Rod Pod or stainless steel telescopic Buzzer Bar (rod holder) and somewhere close to the tip end of the rods, each is balanced and held into a Bite Indicator (an electronic device that sounds a signal to snoozing anglers, or even warns in advance to fellows who are not watching their rod tips) by a line clip.

THE BIG DIFFERENCE

In the wildest stretch of my imagination, I could never of conceived of so huge a difference in styles of carp fishing, from one country to another. Remember, I thought I was an expert, but these fellows have taught me something that will get field tested many, many times. You know what the main difference is between us? ENGLISHMEN DO NOT BAIT THEIR HOOKS!

Big deal, right? Lots of fish are caught in America on LURES! No, uh-uh, I am not talking about lures.

British fishermen catch fish on bait, virtually all of them, but the bait is not on the hook, it is on a piece of line that is attached to the hook! A wild difference, but so simple a one too. The bait is on this piece of line, and we will talk about it further, of course. "Mr. Man" sucks in the bait and in follows the bare hook. If the carp spits the bait out for any reason, the hook usually gets stuck in its lip anyway during the expulsion. If the fish does not exhale the bait, again, a bare hook is in its mouth and very easy to slam into a lip with no food to block the set.

RIGS

English Carpers go about their business with fairly small hooks, maybe size six or so, no different than your fearless writer. They hold bait down with many varieties of Legers (sinkers) and virtually all keep the hook separate from the lead with a barrel swivel. The distance between the barrel swivel and the hook is called a Hooklength (leader). Some rigs are so incredibly complicated that a Boy Scout could earn merit badges learning how to tie them. Read on for some of the many varieties available.

THE REAL DEAL

Remember above, no bait on the hook? Well, a Hair Rig is used to hold the bait. This is light line, mono, or composition, one to two inches long, and bait is threaded onto it by using a Bait Needle. A loop is in the Hair Rig line and it is doubled back, and attached to the hook shank with a plastic device that fastens the bait holding Hair Rig to the hook itself. Think about it. Bait is AT your hook, ingested, and a fish also gets that bare hook in its mouth! Easy to hook that way, right? RIGHT! Did I learn something here? You bet! I hope you did too, and that you practice what our British friends preach.

Tony Broomer told me that the Hair-Rig was invented by famous British Carper, Kevin Maddocks, who used (honest) a hair from his wife's head for the experiment, thus the name!

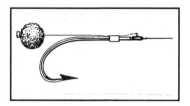

Form of hair-rig with hook.

MORE HELP

Bait is sometimes held at the hook on a Hair Rig with a Boilie Spike (boilie is a bait and a spike keeps it on the "Hair"). PVA string (Poly Vinyl Acetate material that is water soluble) holds objects of chum right at your hook, dissolving in the water but giving nearby carp plenty of Freebie's (oh, we all know what that means).

ANOTHER BIG SECRET — FLOTATION

A Collar of Rubber (traps line) is used with A Waggler (float). Again, the expert admits lack of expertise. Virtually every carp that I have ever caught was AT bottom. I have caught many thousands of other fish well up off of bottom, but I never even tried to fish for carp OFF bottom. Sinker-free or with a sinker, my goal was still to hold the bait within inches of the bottom. I did try for carp with a float many years ago Upstate New York, on the Walkill River, and remember drifting a baited hook downstream a few times before giving it up. Honestly, it was stupid to never try it again, especially once I read how successful this style has proven to be in The U.K.!

I have caught dozens of trout while using a miniature marshmallow at the eye of my hook, and a variety of worms on the hook itself. A foot or two below a sinker, the lead gets to bottom and the marshmallow lifts my worm up a foot or two off bottom, where passing trout can see the food with ease. English anglers use their Hair Rigs sometimes with three or four baits needled on, and a little marshmallow may be threaded between them.

A poly or cork ball is put into play in England at times and Paste (soft bait) is molded around this bit of flotation. The food is held aloft and a Hair keeps the bare hook right in the line of fire of a waiting carp.

CONTINUING

A Trace (wire leader or heavier line) is not often used for carp, but some do go with it to keep the leader from fraying in bottom as it is rubbed across wood or rock. This is more commonly used for pike fishing, to keep a toothy critter from chomping the hook off.

Bolt Rigs (no, not what we did when we were poor, used a heavy bolt instead of a sinker.) An unusual style of fishing for overly fearful carp involves use of a very heavy sinker, at least three ounces, and a long leader. The sinker is held on with a lighter line to your barrel swivel. When a carp picks a bait up and Bolt's (swims off in a big time hurry) away, they often hook themselves by the force of the sudden impact. The lighter line holding the sinker breaks away, and these sinkers are usually non-lead.

Tethered (Snagged in bottom) is an experience that we all fear and experience so many, many a time. A way to get out of some Tether's involves the use of an In-Line sinker and a plastic sleeve that goes over your barrel swivel. Now for our English friends who are getting terribly bored reading about everything they already knew, and for you other Americans', no cheating, but when you get to the section of this book called PINCH-ON, you just may learn something invaluable for your carp escapades. It will be a lesson that every reader can learn from.

CHUM

So much advanced skill is put into use in England, that I just have to tell you about some of the things they do to attract carp to their hooks. Make sure that it is legal to do any of these things though where you live before practicing what they preach. Later for bait itself.

MAGGOT MICHAEL
OF MANCHESTER

Just wait, I'll get to "Chum" itself, first, about Maggot Michael. I received calls from three fishing tackle stores in New Jersey in 1994, all about "Maggot Michael." Remember that the store employees all knew that I was the resident Carp Lunatic. It seemed that Michael was here from England trying to sell a whole new style of fishing, including the use of a slingshot to launch, yuck, MAGGOT's, out into the water for chum. He knew that British carp simply love to eat MAGGOT's, and what better way to encourage Jersey carp to get used to this food than by way of a slingshot launch?

One of the store proprietors put Michael on the telephone with me and we talked about his scheme, and I made an appointment to meet him and watch him in action, at Spruce Run Reservoir, home of thousands of carp. I did casually tell him that a slingshot is a form of an ILLEGAL WEAPON in New Jersey, but no matter, I would gladly watch. He really was upset and when I showed up at the lake, never made his appearance. Maggot Michael of Manchester, I know now that there are legal means of launching Freebies, read on ...

CHUM — CONTINUED

I have caught countless carp with the assistance of chum, and later on, we will talk about chumming, my style. Now though, let's go over some British styles.

Spodding Rods, Throwing Sticks or Bait Bullets (chumlaunchers) are devices that you place chum into and after practice, you can get accuracy plus great distance. Not normally used for maggot launching though, more for heavier chum. Without doubt, the single biggest method used by Englishmen to encourage carp into feeding is to chum a Swim for a day or two before fishing it. Not only does this gather lots of carp to a spot, it also gets them used to the particular kind of bait you will put on your Hair Rig.

Groundbait is a type of chum used to create a cloud of food. It is intended to dissolve and make a slick that fish will follow to your hook. A Feeder Bomb or Frame Feeder is used to mold Groundbait around and cast out, attached to your line. This could be an in-line sinker or some other contraption that chum can be squeezed onto. It works as a continuing chummer for you.

Open Ended Feeders are hollow plastic tubes that contain

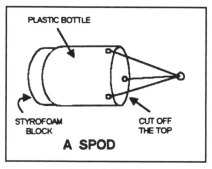

British Spod.

chum at each end. Tied into your line, a slight jerk at the rod every now and then will help release some chum right where you are fishing.

A Spod is an open plastic container, often just a soda bottle, fully loaded with chum. Anglers with great athletic skills tie a heavy line to the Spod and swing it overhead, launching the whole thing way out, to where they hope to fish. Jerking on the line will release the Groundbait onto your Swim and all you need do is cast your hook there.

"Big-Bertha," 18 pound mirror that Tony Broomer stalked for one hour.

BAIT

For full details, please wait for the bait section of the book, but for now, The two basic styles involve big bait or small bait in England. "Boilie's" are the biggies and Particles are the little ones. Later for greater details.

Ah, England. Home of some fat and strangely scaled carp, and many of these fish have their own names! So unique a scale formation have some that steady anglers know Ralph from Sally, and one fish might be caught five to ten times annually. Fat and funny looking, I WANT ONE — PLEASE!

CHAPTER 13

The Law

This chapter will be about as long as the one entitled "Killing And Eating Carp." You see, laws vary from state to state in America, and change as well here and in England and other countries. To say what the law is now would be a mistake in any event, because laws are not constant.

Some states allow chumming, and others may not. We have a few that may not allow the use of corn, for chum, and even for bait. There are people who believe that fish cannot digest corn, and you know that humans have a little difficulty doing so too. On the other hand, I had a friend who personally proved that fish, specifically trout, could digest corn with ease and convinced me that those who felt otherwise did not know what they were talking about.

Several places do not allow the use of more than two fishing rods, the Delaware River, for example. The number of "burr's" per line are also limited on "The Big D."

While I am dead set against it, commercial netting is permitted in various locations too, but for now, let's make up a law that says:

"NO KILLING OF CARP, ANYWHERE, EVER

Wouldn't that be a fine law to have in place, carp lovers?

CHAPTER 14

Boat Angling — Double Anchored

In England, the overwhelming majority of anglers fish from shore, and have developed a vast supply of gadgets to assist in improving their skills. We will talk about fishing from shore, Manny style, in our next chapter but frankly, The "Brit's" have it all over me, save for one thing we will get into in the chapter entitled "PINCH-ON."

Let's first separate this chapter into two basic parts, fishing from a boat in still water, and then in moving water. In many instances, the style stays constant, but there are some variations. First, a lake or pond ...

STILLWATER

Common courtesy, and the desire to avoid being hit in the head by an angry angler's hurled rock, requires fishermen to not always follow my pearls of wisdom on a small and crowded pond. When on a large piece of water without many other boats though, I try to go with a very simple manner of fishing.

While carp are often on the move, and will chase a moving bait, I strongly prefer to have my boat snugged tightly by two anchors at a favorite piece of water. This has worked well for me in many locations, and can produce wonderful results. The best action comes when the wind is modest, but even in a stiff breeze, double anchoring works well.

The good ship "Gone Fishin' " is 1 4.5 feet long, manufactured by Sea Nymph, and is powered by a 9.9 horsepower Evinrude Outboard Motor. Where gasoline engines are not allowed, I use my little Minn-Kota electric kicker for power.

I do not like to fish from a canoe or "John-boat." (A "John-boat" is square in front and low to the water.) I have always felt that they were named for people named John who like to risk death because they are not safe to double-anchor fish from.

To snobs, my boat gives off the appearance that the guy holding the tiller is a rank amateur. No oarlocks are present, nor rod holders. The tin boat has no downriggers, or even seat backs. The entire perimeter of the boat is completely clear of any obstacles, for one good reason. When I go about setting two anchors, I do not want to hang an anchor line in anything in the process, disturbing the otherwise relative quiet I was looking for. Yes, two engines are in the rear, but I can avoid tangles from them because no other line catchers are in the way.

Whether in moving or quiet water, it certainly helps substantially to have prior knowledge of a good area, and clearly, you should have chummed your fishing hole too. A depth finder is a big help to anglers who are on water foreign to them, because as with all fish, drop-off and slope fishing often brings better results. Let's assume that you do everything else correctly beforehand, but you still want to set anchor best for top results.

First, check the wind. Before you go fishing, get as good and accurate a weather report as possible. No, not about rain, about wind direction. What is the prediction for the time you will be on the water, and do they expect a direction change? Generally speaking, there is little or no wind blowing early in the morning, but it will probably crank up eventually, and you need to set your anchors in preparation for it.

You see, you really want one entire side of your boat to be facing the wind. If you position the bow to point into the breeze, then even if perfectly anchored, a swing will occur, causing dirt or mud to be kicked up by the bow anchor, scaring fish away, and flopping around will be present on the stern anchor. Add to that the fact that the boat swinging a bit will also move your lines and I hope you realize that proper wind preparation is critically important.

My boat has two anchors, Danforth-style, and they work well

wherever I go. A Danforth swings on a bar to assist in both anchoring, and releasing later on. The swing will be needed if stuck too well in bottom. To get out, all you need do is go upwind, away from the anchor, to reverse the flukes (points) out of bottom.

Each of my anchors is four pounds, and a four to five foot length of light chain is attached to assist in digging the anchor flukes into the bottom. With a bigger boat, a heavier anchor and chain may be needed. The anchor line itself is ⅜ inch nylon, of fine quality, and at least one hundred fifty feet long. Use of your mother's clothes line or some of that nasty yellow stuff that tangles and splinters after three trips marks the dummy angler who should take up tennis.

There are other anchor types that can be used, obviously. The old cement pail works, as do "Navy Anchors," and grapples. Having used all, I stick with Danforth.

Again, remember where the wind is coming from, OR, will be coming from. Know where you want to fish, and make a slow circle or two to be certain of depth. Position the boat in your mind AND on the water so that when both anchors are set, a whole side will be facing directly into the wind.

Take the bow anchor to your back seat and now put the engine into idle, and then place the bow anchor overboard until it hits bottom. Now put the engine into reverse, going slowly backwards. Let the bow line slip through your fingers and the flukes will dig quickly into bottom, but help by holding the outgoing anchor line, then releasing still more line, ten feet or so at a time. Once you know that you are snug, and have at least an extra fifty feet out, do not stop. This is where most fishermen make their mistake. You cannot set a stern anchor well if you do not have a huge amount of extra line out in the bow.

Continue backing up, until you have released at least one hundred feet of line BEYOND that which was needed to hold bottom, and then, put the engine into neutral.

Let the bow line go slack and now drop the stern anchor overboard until it hits bottom. This process works easier with a friend in the bow, but then again, he may catch some of the fish too so practice going it alone to insure that all the carp that bite hit your baits.

When alone, after the stern anchor has hit bottom, I take the slack line up forward with me and hold a coil or two under my foot on the bow seat. (Remember, no obstacles in the way to get hung up on, starting to make sense now?) Then I grab the bow anchor line and start pulling it in, until the stern line begins to tighten. Here we will need experience, but if you do it three or four times, you will get it right, trust me.

Continue pulling on the bow line and then release ten feet on the stern, and then stamp down to start to dig the stern anchor flukes into bottom. Take in another ten feet up forward, releasing ten more to the rear, and again, stop the stern line with your shoe. Are you starting to get the picture?

The stern line will not get into bottom as easily as the bow, but with this process, it will work. Pulling the boat from the bow will do it, if you coordinate your bow pull properly with your stern release and stop, trust me!

Once both anchors are into bottom, and each has fifty extra feet or so of line out ("scope"), tie both lines securely to the boat, bow and stern, and tighten each as well as possible. If there will be little or no wind, your boat will hardly shift at all and you can fish either side of the boat in extreme comfort, knowing that your lines will be right there with your chum, if you did it all correctly.

Fishing can get rather exciting with a large carp hooked and your boat set up with two anchors, but even though most large carp will eventually charge the boat and go under it, I have never lost a carp to an anchor line. If you have too little scope out, a carp could give you a mono-breaking turn around that line, but with plenty of anchor line out, you should be able to let the fish go under or around. You may also assist in leading the beast too, if not too large.

MOVING WATER

It is far easier to set two anchors in moving water, unless the current is very fast. Than it may be near to impossible. Carp are

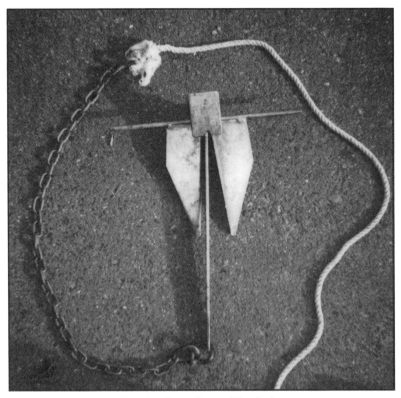

Danforth anchor with chain.
Quality line is attached with a poor quality knot!

not easy to catch in rapid water anyway, so let's just assume that you are in a river or stream that is not chugging too swiftly.

A different variety of anchor is available for rivers, called aptly, a "River-Anchor." It has three or four flukes, not as long as a Danforth, and does not have any moving parts. This anchor gets into bottom, behind rocks, or wood, and sometimes is easier to release from bottom at the end of your trip. Frankly though, I still prefer a Danforth.

Setting into bottom here is not much different than in a lake, but instead of using wind direction to get a whole side facing wind, just make sure you get a whole side to face UPCURRENT. This can get tricky if there is a stiff wind blowing from one side of the boat, or worse, from downstream, but generally, the current will get you positioned just fine.

You need to set one anchor pointing towards a shoreline and then back up and do it again with the second anchor facing the other shore. I often do not even need to get that fancy in current. Just chuck one anchor over upstream and then the other. If two anglers or one, getting both anchors dug in should be an easy task. You want to wind up with enough extra line out at either end to have a secure bite into bottom.

Done correctly, I have been able to fish as many as eight lines overboard, all facing downcurrent. Yes, maybe the boat looks like a Battleship, but it works.

Whatever you do, make sure the tag ends of your anchor lines are tied to the boat, because once you put an anchor in and release all your line and watch the end slip into the water, something magical occurs and the line will never be seen again. If you do this, you will then become a "single-anchor" fisherman, and someone trying to catch carp from a boat that is flopping around on a single anchor is a sorry sight indeed.

―――――――

CHAPTER 15

Shore Angling

Here we must face England and take a deep bow. Again, the folks of Great Britain have studied the science of carp angling and since most of their fishing is done from shore, they really know how to do it. For the first twenty of my forty plus years of carp angling, virtually all of the carp that I caught were from shore, but again, the fellows across the pond do it far better than we do in the States.

We have already discussed carp fishing in England, so I will not repeat what you have read. Instead, let me try to explain the basic details that need be known to find yourself tied to the other end of a carp from shore.

For openers, probably half the lakes and rivers in America hold carp, but before fishing a venue, do talk to the local tackle store owner to make certain that you are after Rubberlips where he really does swim. You could wind up wasting a lot of time catching trash fish like smallmouth bass on your corn kernels, or a good-for-nothing monster channel catfish. Someone I know even caught a 10 pound northern pike on a half-dozen niblits.

Now that you know that the water holds carp, next is finding some legal and ample standing room. There may be many places where you are allowed to fish from, but the clearing may be insufficient to fight a fish up and down the bank.

If the fish runs to the left and a stand of trees is blocking your running path, kiss that baby goodbye, unless you run into the water and around the trees! Even worse is a large overhanging tree.

Good buddy Ron Bern, author of the South Carolina chapter

found herein, and the person who helped make my "Carp in the Bathtub" chapter easier for you to understand, was the cause of major concern for me one fine day on the Delaware River, and that experience proved that you really need a lot of standing and running room, or else you had better have a lunatic for a friend.

Now Ron had not yet caught his first carp in New Jersey, but had been with me and watched as I took a dozen or two, in both the Raritan and Delaware Rivers. Suffice it say therefore that he really, really needed to catch a carp.

The location was the Delaware, and we were upstream of the little town of Byram. The clearing was very small, unfortunately, and Ron had a "double figure" fish at the other end of his line.

Needless to say, the fish hung him up around a branch that stuck over into the water, and it was a tug of war for man and beast, and the beast was winning.

Your fearless writer figured that losing his first carp could really mess Bern up, big time, so I told him to hang onto the rod, and I walked out into the water, fully clothed, and got Ron's line free. Somehow I managed to get back on dry land without killing myself and shortly, the carp became Ron's. He released it, of course, but Bern's first New Jersey carp weighed better than 10 pounds.

Shore angling needs clear dirt underfoot too. If you are standing in heavy weed it can be murder to run back and forth while chasing a fish and keep from getting your legs all tangled up. Even funnier is to have to slosh through mud en route. Some very fine ballet steps were surely invented by carp anglers flying through the air after hitting a pile of goo.

The methods used for positioning your rods, very important for shore anglers, will be talked about later on, as will the use of drag vs. open bales, etc. For now though, the key to shore angling for carp remains SPACE. Without enough running room to your left and right, you can generally figure that more than half the carp you hook will either break you off in a snag of some sort, or just get away while you are slipping and sliding.

CHAPTER 16

Rods n' Reels

Here again, we in America have been humbled by our friends in England! British carp anglers use reels similar to those I favor, but bigger! The same thing applies to their rods, but with even a greater difference. Generally speaking, it is spinning rods and reels in Great Britain, and my preference runs in the same direction. The basis difference though is that I use far lighter stuff!

We have spoken about the ten to 12 foot stiff sticks used in English "swim's." These are matched with smooth running reels that have the widest opening drags possible. Shimano or Silex "Bait-Runner's" are tops. Again, no basic difference, other than size. I like Daiwa reels too, and of course, the old standby, Penn is dependable. My garage has six Fenwick Rods and another 20 or so other rods hanging from ceiling hooks.

I have seen carp fishermen throwing bait out with saltwater surf spinning gear to reach their quarry far offshore. This requires use of heavier line and while I like to catch fish, big fish, frankly, the heavy stuff is not for me. I would rather not go after carp if it meant using 15-20 pound mono or more and a big "Meat Stick."

Carp are known to swim to the other side of the lake or river, if you let them. This is why long and stiff rods are used in England. Since most of my fishing is done from a boat though, I have the opportunity of chasing a fish if it swims too far away. Yes, the anchors need to be pulled but if a big "Mr. Man" is on the hook, I might do just that.

Many people like to use modern day bait casting gear. The

rods are stiffer and the drags do run smoothly, but casting is far more difficult other than for the pro's. Another major difference to me though is the DRAG SOUND. There are few bait casting reels on the market that make a sound that is adequate for my taste.

The screech of drag, protesting in vain against the rush of a racing carp is what I want to hear, what I yearn for every trip, and bait casting reels do not give me that pleasure. In addition, if my back is turned or I am on shore and away from the rod, a Big-Scaler could be running line off the revolving spool reel without my even having had a single clue about it.

Match your rod and reel, clearly. An ultra-lite rod and reel combination will do just fine. Yes, you may get hung up more because you lose control, but we are after fun too, not just a "score."

Without doubt, the folks who say that they just want the fresh air, or maybe just want to hook a fish, or perhaps need only see the critter to count it as a great day, are LIARS, or worse yet, FOOLS! I want to catch my fish, but still want to go light.

I want a reel with a drag adjustment that is on top of the reel, not under or behind it. The top turning drag reel is one that has a sound that is more true. Those reels with drag adjustments below the reel have disappointed me often. After a sufficient number of drag screamers, the sound disappears. There is a tiny bit of metal inside these reels that separates itself from the device that causes the sound after a while. If you cannot hear the drag, it could be murder trying to fight a fish because you may just be turning the handle against the fish without gaining line. This makes for the worst kinds of twists and tangles in your line.

My boat always has a five foot ultra-lite in it, plus a six foot medium weight rod, and I do have a few seven footers also. I keep away from the "slow action" (stiff) rods because I simply prefer the medium's. Long "fast action" (very whippy) rods are not at all good either because you lose all control that way.

Balancing your gear is most important and buying quality equipment, plus maintaining it that way with periodic examinations of guides to make sure no cuts have been worn in is critical. Proper lubrication of each reel is important, and NEVER use a carp reel in saltwater. Your line will not work properly again in a lake or river, no matter how well you wash the reel.

Two guys holding what probably would be a state record for Connecticut — 52 pounds, but they didn't officially record their catch!

CHAPTER 17

Terminal Tackle

This chapter will deal with the kind of gear that you have to use along with your rods and reels. No matter how high the quality of the R & R's, without proper terminal tackle-line, hooks, sinkers, etc., forget catching carp!

Here again we bow towards the British Isles where so vast an array of equipment is used. Frankly, I do believe that I have personally learned a great deal to improve my carp catching skills during the research I did in producing this book. Dan Gapen's book, as well as Edwin Cooper's, and those from England, taught me far more than what I knew before.

My own style has stayed somewhat constant over the years, save for one basic element. I have eliminated the use of treble hooks and gone strictly to the use of single's.

Let's go over the items that will help you catch carp.

HOOKS: Once upon a time, before I discovered the wonders of kernel corn in moving water, the hook was a treble hook, used to hold cooked corn meal on better than a single hook could. In fact we used to use a treble hook that had a wire contraption running around its shank and this wire held the bait on quite well indeed. The sizes varied from 4 to 8 depending on how large a ball of bait I wanted to use. Generally speaking though, size six was standard. The major problem with using a treble hook is that it is three times easier to get hung up into bottom! Once we began to use corn in rivers (I always used it in lakes) I got rid of the trebles and now use just singles, even for corn meal balls.

Now that I have partially gone away from cooked corn meal,

my hook of choice is a number 6 or 8 Eagle Claw style with bait holder. The two barbs on the shank of the hook ("the bait holders") work well to keep the bait on. This helps hold corn meal, boilie, or the four to six kernels of corn that I generally use, and also does the trick with other baits such as a worm.

What your fearless writer must now do is practice what the English carp anglers preach, the use of "hair-rigs" and such, to eliminate the need to actually put any bait at all on your hook itself. Again, friends, this concept is so wildly unique and different that I cannot wait to try it.

The key to catching carp, whether you bait your hook itself or not, is to use a very strong piece of steel. Thin wired hooks will be bent into straight pins by the rush of a "double-figure," and that could ruin your whole day!

SINKERS: Sorry, but here I must say that no matter what kind of sinkers others may use anywhere else, there is only one primary sinker to use, ONE, UNO, EIN, I, 1, PERIOD! That sinker is an egg or barrel shaped one with holes at both ends so that you can cast well, but still let your carp run away without knowing someone is at the other end of the bait.

When we get to the PINCH-ON chapter, I will talk to you further about what I view as the supreme difference that exists between my style and the English style, one that everyone will learn makes for a major improvement in their skill.

Of course the best weight to use is your bait itself. If you do not have to cast far, no weight is the best weight. This greatly assists in catching carp because even if you are using a few split shot sinkers, that weight could be felt. As a youngster, fishing Prospect Park Lake in Brooklyn, we used to run a dozen kernels of corn up the line and add four or so more to the hook itself. A good rod, with reel filled with light line could cast out as far as one hundred feet and this worked the best of all.

To repeat, a quarter to two ounce egg/barrel sinker, PERIOD! A pinch-on (split-shot) too, but later for that.

SWIVEL: Sure now that my friends who drive on the wrong side of the road will yell and scream, dear friends, the only kind of swivel to use is NO SWIVEL AT ALL. Again, when we get to PINCH-ON, you will learn, trust me, that the bald guy from Brooklyn is right.

LINE: I keep away from processed lines, even though their diameters are so much thinner than standard monofiliment. A ten pound carp screaming drag away can cut a truly fine grove in your finger if you are using "Ironthread" or such. Get a digit in the way of that train at the other end and while mono could scratch your finger, the other lines could make you into "four-finger!"

I use good quality mono, six or eight pound test, and change it often, line that is never used in saltwater because that ruins the lay of the line on bottom. While heavier line surely improves your chances of beating a big fish, my own experience has proven to me that, especially in some of our more clear waters, light is best. No, I keep away from two to four pound line, that really is a bit much.

I always use two different line colors. Pink for six pound test and my eight pound is white. Frankly, I think that blue, green, gray or that silly orange-glow-in-the dark stuff takes away from my luck. The reason for the two that I do use with color varieties is simple, although not at first. Think about it though. The way I figure it, if I look at a reel and see pink, I know that the line on that spool is six pound test, and may need more ease in fighting the fish. White means eight pound to me, and here I have one-third more fighting strength.

Fishing close to shore or near to the boat, I use the reel(s) with six pound to disguise my presence better. The sticks that brought me further away contain white eight pound test.

No, I am not a brain-dead old fool either. I own thirty or more reels and could not be certain which reel contains what test line without this simple method.

Our chapter on England tells you a great deal about many

other items of terminal tackle and rather than repeating, let me just refer you back to that chapter.

Most importantly though, they use one manner or another of a "Bite-Indicator," generally one that is electronic. The sound of drag is just fine, but why not go electronic too? Other bite-indicators used are little aluminum bits and pieces, held onto your rod tip by a partially straightened out paper clip. Yet one more is a simple piece of tissue paper held on the line by, sorry, a touch of spit. Holding a coil or two of spare line on the ground with a bit of cooked corn meal/boilie or a little twig works too.

CHAPTER 18

Bait

The truth be known, I have only caught carp on six varieties of bait, even though people all over the world can put together a list many times that. Let's first talk about the baits that I have used, and then about some of the others.

MANNY BAIT

CORN KERNEL. While catfish, bass, sunfish, chub and roach have bothered me from time to time while using corn, I still prefer to use anywhere from four to six kernels of it on a hook. Will I also try it out on a hair-rig? You bet!

There are many anglers who like to flavor their corn overnight in a variety of scents. If you want to know the truth — I never thought of it, but sure will try. We will talk about only a few of the many flavors available in the next bait type.

Some folks prefer dried feed corn and buy it in large bags, taking out enough to use as chum and bait for each outing, adding appropriate smell as well. These kernels are softened and saturated by what they are allowed to sit in overnight. In addition to getting smell, the kernels become easier for carp to both ingest AND digest this way.

If you go with canned corn, the big lesson here is to carefully examine the can before you leave the supermarket. I actually went fishing one day with two cans, one for bait and the other for chum, but failed to read the labels. Each can contained cream-style corn! There were smiling carp a long way downstream that day, drinking in the chum, but I had no kernels at all for bait. Fortunately, I did have some corn meal, and caught some carp!

CORN MEAL. There are two basic colors, before adding anything else. More normally used is yellow meal, but also available is white.

Eastern European people used to call cooked corn meal "Mommah-Liggah," and it was a staple in the diet of many, especially those with little money. Another use for corn meal as food is called "Polenta," and fine Italian Restaurants provide this often as the starch to accompany your meat in America.

For now, let's feed carp, not people, okay? The jury is really out on whether it is better to make up the bait and then boil it, or to mix and cook the bait in a pot. In England, the style involves taking a mixture of additives, blending them in with the raw meal, maybe adding flour, and balling the whole deal up. THEN they boil the ball. This bait is called "BOILIE'S" and we will get to that shortly.

My method of preparing corn meal bait is to take a standard kitchen pot and put a small glass of water in it. It really is trial and error until you do it often enough to need no written instructions. Standing by me are the following:

1. Boxes of yellow and white corn meal.
2. A container of flour.
3. Sugar.
4. Extra water.
5. Flavors like Vanilla Extract, Anise, Cocoa, Strawberry Jello, chopped onion, and chopped garlic. The "sky is the limit," but for now, start with these.
6. Several large table spoons and a teaspoon.
7. A few pieces of aluminum foil.

I boil the water, and then throw in three to four tablespoonfuls of yellow meal and another of flour, turning the stove burner down half-way to avoid burning everything. Quickly following is a dash of vanilla extract, and a teaspoon of sugar. Now here is where the mad scientist takes over. No one can talk to me as I mix and mash the whole mess, carefully making sure that there are no dry spots of meal. If the spoon cannot be moved, the bait is too dry and I add some water. Again, trial and error. Add more vanilla for smell, and make sure that the consistency of the bait is smooth, but not too soft.

If you think you may have it right, take everything out of the pan and place it in a half-dozen or so hunks onto one of the small sheets of aluminum foil that you have ready. Quickly lift one hunk and knead it with your hands into what appears to be something that feels like it will stay on your hook (or "Hair-Rig.") Once you know the feel, you will remember it, trust me. Take another piece of bait and repeat the process. Once each part of the bait is hand-mixed, then ball all the parts up together tightly and wrap it in aluminum. This can hold a good consistency in your refrigerator for several days.

Never go with just one flavored ball. Try white meal with anise. Maybe white with onion. Perhaps yellow with cocoa, and so on. Before I discovered that corn kernels worked well in rivers, I used to take at least three or four different balls of "Mommah-Liggah" with me. We used to use corn in lakes alone but now find that it is often better than corn meal in rivers too. The basic difference is that when corn meal is eaten, it usually is in the mouth of "Mr. Man," and kernels are eaten by most fish that swim!

The best thing about "Mommah-Liggah" to me, besides the obvious, is that my nose just loved to inhale most of the scents as I cooked my bait, preparing me and getting my fishing juices boiled along the way. An "Adrenalin Rush?" Well, no, but a jump start to Carping, for sure.

By the way, buy your own pot or maybe two. Such a container should never be used for people food, because it is nearly impossible to clean one. Besides, you WANT your own pot!

DOUGHBALL: Mix dough, water, and flavor, and this need not be cooked at all to hold consistency. This bait has been used for carp as long as carp have been in America, and it still works. I still prefer to cook it with corn meal though.

*Chef Luftglass cooking up
a mess of Walkill Mommah-liggah back in 1954.*

WORMS: Springtime brings moving water, and moving water brings worms into the water. Therefore some of the best carp bait in the spring can be the common worm. We have lots of varieties to pick from, and most are carp food. Some people think that carp are vegetarians, but this is not at all true.

Darkened water is best for carp with worm, as well as flood-heightened waters. I have even caught carp on worm in the summer right after a heavy downpour of rain. The earliest carp I ever took in cold water was on March 1st and that nine pounder went for a night crawler worm.

CRAWFISH: Not many, but I did catch a few carp in Prospect Park Lake in Brooklyn many years ago on "crayfish." — No, not the whole live crawfish, you need to remove the tail section, peel as you might do with a lobster, and just put the meat on your hook. Here, as with worms and corn, watch for other critters that will to try and eat your bait first.

BREAD: Floating bread has worked all over the world ever since the first carp was caught. There are several lakes on Staten Island in New York City where specialists use a piece of (HONEST) poppy seed bagel, cast out and left to float on top. I caught carp in Brookville Park, Rosedale, Queens, in the fifties and sixties, using a small piece of common white or rye bread.

The problem with floating bread or bagel, besides it being tough to get far from shore, is that ducks and gulls have no respect at all. Many times they will eat the offering before a carp can suck it in. Then the best part begins though because just picture a drunk stumbling by as you are fighting a bird overhead. It could cure him forever!

LIVE FISH: Well, only one, and it was quite a surprise. I was fishing for hybrid bass at Spruce Run Reservoir in Clinton, New Jersey, with a five inch alewife herring on a sinker-free hook when the drag went off. Rearing back on the rod, I stuck the barb into a six pound carp!

That pretty well sums up my own carp baits, but read on ...

OTHER AMERICAN BAIT

POWER BAIT: Made by the Berkley people, this is intended for trout, but a 47 pound mirror carp, the new State Record, was caught in 1995 in New Jersey by a young man on Power Bait.

PREPARED CARP BAIT: Uncle Josh, for one, is a brand name

of bait that can be found on the counters of tackle stores all over America. Many think that it is as good as or better than any bait you prepare yourself, and much less work.

POTATO: Frankly, I tried it, and never had so much as a bite. Dan Gapen, author of "Why Fish Carp" swears by the use of a partially boiled potato. Try small whole potatoes or a large cut portion of a bigger one. There are few other fish that care much about this food, other than, maybe catfish, so what use of potato generally accomplishes is that when you get a bite, it nearly always is "Puckerpuss."

MULBERRIES: Find a live Mulberry Tree with ripe fruit, overhanging a slow moving or still piece of water that contains carp, and you will definitely find carp under the tree, sucking in each berry as it falls into the water. Here is where you want to "match the hatch," using a few of the berries on your hook.

ENGLISH BAIT

BOILIES: Many English anglers do not bother making their own bait. They have hundreds of varieties of prepared carp bait available to them, in bait-sized balls, generally in air-tight bags. This bait is mixed, balled, and then boiled to give proper consistency. Again, I mix, boil and lastly, ball. Which stays better? There's may stay longer, but I think mine presents a bait that is easier to ingest.

Reading from "David Hall's Advanced Carp Fishing," two kinds are called Strawberry Cream and Cranberry Nutrafruit. The magazine, "Carpworld" offers, among others, Old English Toffee, Tutti Frutti, and Frankfurter Sausage. Darn near anything you can think of, and then some, may be added.

NATURALS: A good name, used for anything alive, no doubt. Worms, for sure, but also maggot's, and many other small living creatures that can find themselves into the water. If it floats or sinks, you can bet that carp may just like to eat it. We often see carp boiling on top and while sometimes they are spawning, and other times, maybe just playing, why not the possibility of them eating insects and the like up on top?

PARTICLES: Corn, mostly, like used in America, but also peas, beans and anything else that can be laced onto a hair-rig.

GROUNDBAIT: Simple enough, this stands for bait that is ground up! The bait is mixed into a mass and then molded onto different kinds of objects, called "Feeders." Cast well out, with hook, hair-rig, etc., also attached, the "Feeder" actually does just that, it feeds the groundbait to carp. Bits and pieces of the ground up bait fall off, or are pecked off, and eventually, a carp will then see the larger "Boilie" inches away, and eat and get caught.

In deep dark basements, all over Europe, the Orient, and the United States, there surely are some people mixing and mashing, inventing yet more combinations to feed to carp.

CHAPTER 19

Chum

Perhaps as critically important as anything else in the bag of tricks of an expert carp angler is his ability to attract fish to a location by use of "Chumming." My handy dandy little Webster's New World Dictionary defines the word chum as meaning "a close friend." Next it says that chumming is "to be close friends." Well, that about sums it up, doesn't it?

Whether you are after tuna or trout, shark or catfish, fish just like to eat and eat. If you can attract fish to the area you are going to work, you have a giant step up on the path towards a successful day. Befriend a carp — feed it!

I have already told you about "Maggot Michael of Manchester," a fellow who was trying to promote the use of slingshots. He would launch maggots out to a chosen spot in a lake to attract carp to the lines that would also be baited with maggots. His concept was sound other than the little problem of use of slingshots in New Jersey being illegal. The English have invented other methods of propelling chum and among them is a quite legal device called a Spod.

It is easier to catapult chum out with a slingshot, but with proper practice, you can do so too with a Spod, and pin-point accuracy can even be achieved after a while when the wind is not blowing hard.

Chumming for carp is done before you fish, or even while you are fishing. An area is loaded with chum for days before fishing sometimes, some each day until you are ready to heave out your own lines.

It is much easier to chum a lake or pond because the food falls and stays put. Throwing freebies out onto a river or stream can be tricky because the current will take it out.

SHORE CHUMMING: Putting free food into the water by boat before you fish is most sensible, and so many methods can be used, but if you are fishing from shore, the list is cut down. From shore, again, some launching method is needed.

BOAT CHUMMING: I much prefer to fish from a boat, and while this style is not available everywhere, for those who can do so, let's talk to them for now.

If you are really after carp, take the time to pick your spot ("swim") beforehand, marking where you will anchor up in your eyes with shoreline readings. Oh you know, about so many feet downstream of the green house on one shore, and this many below the fallen tree on the other bank, etc.

Determine how far away from one river bank you will do your fishing from, and then liberally put your chum into the water in a good area, as close to exactly where you think your lines will be when you go fishing. This can be done the same day you fish too, without anchoring your boat. It requires the use of an electric motor for quiet, or better, oars. Two people improve your chances. One controls the boat and the other puts the freebies into the drink.

You have to account for current in moving water. Lighter chum will wash away quickly, but anything with substance will remain where you put it, if heavy enough.

It is far easier to chum an area on a lake. Just pin-point where you will anchor with land bearings and then take slow and quiet circles around that place, chumming as you go.

Three or four days in a row before your fishing trip is normally enough time to prepare a "swim." Fish will gather and stay, waiting for food, and do try to use chum in flavors similar to what you will put on your hook or hair-rig. "Matching the hatch," or duplicating the chum, is what you are after. Sure, carp will hit many kinds of bait but why not let them get used to what you will bait with?

WHILE FISHING

While fishing in current, I will always throw some corn kernels upstream of my boat, so that they will slowly move down to where my waiting hooks are. If the current is really running, do not bother to use corn as chum because it will wind up feeding fish a half-mile downstream.

Chumming with softened cooked corn meal will work well in both moving and still water. Heavy enough to stay put, or maybe just move very slowly with current, again, make sure to use "Mommah-Liggah," or "Boilie's" in the scent that you will try to hook your fish with.

Some folks like to chum with an attachment tied directly to their fishing line! A "chum-feeder" is a device that meal, mash, etc., can be molded around and cast out, with baited line tied in. The feed will be released into the water, attracting fish to the hookbait.

A variety of "Chum-feeder" may be your sinker itself. A hollow aluminum container, which can be opened for insertion of a glob of chum and screwed closed is a fine method. Way back in the fifties we used to use something quite similar for winter flounder. We placed some cat food, ground up mussels or clams, etc., into the sinker, and dropped it in with baited hooks below. The chum-sinker would attract flounder to the baited hooks.

MAGGOT CHICKEN: Now that really doesn't sound very tasty, does it? Well, to carp it could be something like "Meals on Wheels!" I have heard that some people will tie a dead chicken to an overhanging tree branch and simply let the bird remain there until it starts to spoil. The warmer the weather, the quicker this occurs. After a day or two, maggots, yuck, will inhabit the corpse and do what maggots do, multiply and eat. Some will fall into the water, close to shore, and underneath will be those beautiful toothless mouths, sucking the freebies in.

MAGGOT FISHHEADS: A variation on the above system, really. I spoke to a top New Jersey fisherman who I knew late in

January of 1996, Walter Neumann, about my forthcoming book. He told me that in his native country, Germany, they used to tie the head of a fish to an overhanging branch too. This was done where a quick drop-off existed and the water was three to four feet deep very close to shore. The nasty little maggots would invade the head eventually and then become living chum as they dropped off into the water.

British anglers call fishing right near shore "Margin" fishing, and these chumming styles are perfect for going after these carp. Just a few maggots on your hook, no sinker needed, and a "Bugle-mouth" will suck them in.

Befriend a carp, feed it well with chum, and go catch 'em!

CHAPTER 20

Lures

As someone who specializes in the use of bait for 99% of the fish that I seek, I must admit to not having taken a single carp on a lure. That does not mean, however, that carp have not been caught that way.

Without doubt, anglers seeking shad in the Delaware River with a little shad dart or flutter spoon snag into some carp by accident from time to time. Some of the carp that are caught by shad fishermen are even hooked in the mouth. Now does the carp go after the lure to eat it, or to chase it away? In fact, does the critter go after the lure at all or is it accidentally hooked in the mouth as the barb passes by?

Fly rod users too will get their hairy or fuzzy offerings stuck into the rubber lips of a Big-Scaler sometimes. Did you ever see a ten pound carp tear line away from a single action fly reel? Called "knuckle busters," a fly reel screeching out in reverse with Mr. Man running downstream is quite a sight and sound.

In fact years ago, I fished for carp often with fly tackle, but the reel contained 100 yards of eight pound test monofiliment, and I was always using corn meal balls with no sinker at all instead of a fly. My best carp on such gear was a 12 pounder on the Walkill River at Montgomery, N.Y. Although this was forty years ago, I can remember virtually the entire experience.

To digress, casting a pile of mono coils that are laid on the ground, through your guides, is quite a task, especially in a wind. Maybe that is why I don't fish that way any longer.

There really are fly rodders who purposely fish for carp and my guess is that many of the fish that are seen sucking in flies in waters that contain trout, bass and carp, are the carp instead of the first two. Some carp go for flies on the surface, as they fall into the water. Still others pick off those that are rising up off bottom during a hatch.

Author and tackle manufacturer Dan Gapen holding 22 pounder caught on an Ugly Bug.

Writer Dan Gapen swears by the use of Ugly Bug lures. Their rubber legs and soft body make them a crawfish look-alike and carp eat crawfish, especially the soft-shelled variety. He writes that he has used brown Ugly Bug's in the summer, especially in the Mississippi River.

Does a carp hit a jig or does the jig hit the carp? Frankly, whatever gets the fish hooked, they still fight like all get out. I do not go out of my way though to fish for carp with lures. Bait works just too well for me!

CHAPTER 21

What Time?

COLD WATER

When fishing in cold water, I feel that carp are better sought after during the middle part of the day, especially when the sun is out. A few degree difference in surface water temperature can make a carp start to think about food. Forgetting the additional comfort of a few hours more sleep, try starting your trip at noon instead of shivering your way to the water at 5 a.m.!

SPRINGTIME

Since mid-spring seems to be the time that carp really get serious about eating, the spring is when to really work at fishing for them, and darn near anytime is carp time in the spring. Fishing from shore, I prefer very early, starting even before sunup. I have caught lots of carp from shore, close in, until ten a.m., and sometimes all day long. Things get better again about two hours before dark, but spring carp generally slow down at dark.

If fishing a river from my boat, I like inshore still, but by 9 a.m. or so, I am out to mid-river, to the deepest water I can find and for some reason, 9:30 to 11 in the morning is when I do my best.

SUMMERTIME

Boat and other traffic causes inshore carp to chase way out early each morning, and excessive water temperature moves them out in any event. While I do catch carp inshore very early each day, it is often all over by 7 in the morning. This is when it is important to fish far offshore. Boat anglers have it all over the land-based guys as a result.

Many of my carp have been taken during the dark of the night in the summer. The water temperature gets more comfortable, but again, I think that carp like the improvement in quiet. Between water skiers, speedboats, jet-skis and who knows what else that scares them into a non-feed mode, night time may very well be the best time.

AUTUMN

The fall is a fine time to fish for carp, but not nearly as good as spring or summer. Bigger carp are taken in the fall, but not nearly as many. The biggies need to eat more to fatten up and prepare for the shut down in eating that occurs as water temperature drops. Especially in colder states, carp hardly eat anything after November, until April, unless the food is within inches of its nose, or you are at a warmwater discharge on a river.

Try to fish for carp in the autumn between 8 a.m. and noon.

SOLUNAR TIME

What does this mean? Honestly, I do not know the true meaning but Solunar time relates to position of moon and sun. For some reason, carp, and most other fish, get into bigger feeding moods based on this positioning. In fact, many hunters too swear by "The Original Knight" Solunar Table to assist in determining when to get their guns ready.

I have found that following the Solunar Table, at least 80% of the time IN STILL WATER, carp, AND many other fish, eat like the dickens! Even in the middle of a hot day in the summer, I have caught many trout, carp, etc., during a peak Solunar Period.

You can probably pick up a Solunar chart somewhere, and it will tell you which four periods of every day are better than the rest of the day. There will be a thirty minute period (Minor peak) and a 90–120 minute Major peak in the first 12 hours of the day. The next 12 hours will again see a minor and major time period.

A dramatic change in wind or barometer will generally mess up the feeding pattern and throw out that day's Solunar prediction, but without either change, IT WORKS! The hot action time STARTS at the time shown, it does not surround same. In other words, if the major peak time on the morning of Sunday, January 21, 1996 was shown as 11:40 a.m., that was when the 90–120 minute peak started!

The Solunar Table works well too in rivers, and even in saltwater, but my best results come in lakes and ponds.

VIBRATION TIME

When a fish is feeding, it gives off vibrations in the water. We all know that live bait trying to escape from an open mouth does not do too well because the vibrations that they release in their rush to survive make the critters that are after them even more crazed. I feel, and have personally proven to myself that it is true, that feeding fish create more feeding fish!

I am not just talking about a school of predators chasing through wildly jumping baitfish. That is a no-brainer. A single fish, going after a bait, even dead bait or cooked bait, gets the interest up in nearby fish to do the same.

Yes, we have all been hit by two fish within seconds of each other when each line is a few feet from the other. Big deal! That is probably two or more feeding fish that are swimming together. No, I am talking about two fish hitting different lines that are separated by dozens of feet, and generally, this involves two different times for each bite, moments apart. Once the first fish runs drag, you stick it, and another line goes off. Did the first fish create vibrations in the water that made the pea-brain of the second fish say to itself, "Self, EAT!" In my opinion, yes, absolutely.

Over the years I have had hundreds of second fish hit my offering a long distance away from fish number one within moments. Did the second fish swim like a nut to find food to eat BECAUSE it got the message from fish number one? In my opinion, YES!

CHAPTER 22

Pinch-On
(The Biiig Difference)

I n reading four English publications that deal with carp fishing, plus several books printed in America, as well as the fine newsletter put out by our Carp Anglers Group, I failed to see one thing. One little teenie tiny item, that is missing, and to me, it really is THE BIIIG DIFFERENCE!

It is commonly known that carp are very smart critters, and that the best weight to use while fishing for them is no weight at all. Taking a bait that is not anchored at all by any lead is the best way to catch carp. However, the need for distance, or the requirement to hold bait down in current, requires most anglers to use some manner of sinker.

Over the forty plus years that I have fished for carp, I must have gotten stuck in bottom, be it under a rock or around a large tree branch, etc., about a gadillion (that's a lot) times! This obviously happens to anglers everywhere, and many methods have been used to escape that snag.

THAT DOGGONE SWIVEL

Every system that I have seen written about involves some manner or another of a two-way barrel swivel. Clearly, use of a swivel substantially cuts down on line twist as you turn the handle of your reel, especially while fighting a beast of a carp. On the other hand, if weight is needed, the swivel IS NOT NEEDED!

I have seen some remarkable pictures of rigs put together by Carpers in Great Britain. They ALL involve a small dark barrel swivel. This stops your sinker above it, and allows the leader below to hold your hook, with hair-rig, and gosh knows what other wonderful inventions that induce a carp to eat.

Light lines that contain chumming devices are tied into the main line, either at the top loop of the barrel swivel, or even at the bottom loop. The top of the barrel may also have your heavy weight attached on a light line to assist in break off. If this lighter line gets hung in bottom, no problem, it will break away. That leaves your hook, hopefully in the mouth of a carp, and you are clear to fight your fish — — or maybe not!

HUNG

To repeat, unless the bottom of your venue is clear of all kinds of obstructions, we, all of us, everywhere, will get hung often. This takes place by your sinker rolling a bit on bottom, in wind, or current. It occurs so many times while simply reeling in, unless you retrieve line so quickly with rod tip held high that you are lucky enough to escape the various hang-ups that are between you and the place where you cast to.

The worst kind of snag to get into is the one that a carp finds for you. This could happen accidentally, or the smart Big-Scaler could take you there on purpose. Carp know where to go to do this. They may even have a map that they consult from time to time during quiet winter months to refresh their memories. If there is a log, tree branch, or groups of submerged rocks, Mr. Man knows where they are. The bigger the carp, the more snags that he will take you to. Whether you get stuck permanently depends on a few things — skill, luck, and very importantly — A PINCH-ON!

THE PINCH-ON

We have all used little split-shot (pinch-on) sinkers in our life. Trout fishermen use one to four of them of varied size while bouncing a salmon egg downstream. The sinker is round, and has a crack in the center, running more than half-way through. Place the little lead in your hand, slit up, and put your line in the slot, and pinch the lead closed around the line.

Some use their own fingers, and other fishermen feel that a

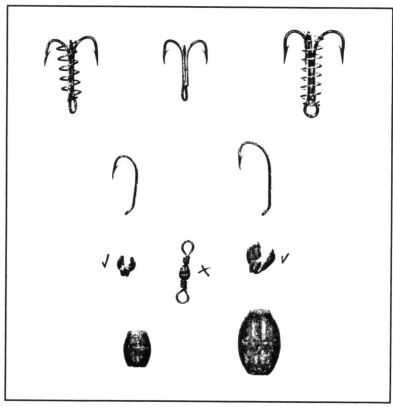

Top (left to right): #6 coiled, #8 regular, #4 coiled trebles.
Next, #'s 8 & 6 Eagle Claws with bait-holder.
Line three: little shot, bottom-snagging swivel, larger shot.
Lastly, ¼ and ½ ounce egg sinkers.

pair of fishing pliers is better to get a tighter closing. Again, so very simple, and we have all done this often, WITHOUT heavier lead. Years back, pinch-ons were perfectly round, and could only be used one time. For the past twenty or thirty years, they are now also available with a little collar that allows you to open the closed lead and either remove the sinker or move it up or down on your line.

WHAT GETS STUCK?

If I have gotten stuck in bottom once, I have been nailed to something tens of thousands of times over the years. My guess is that ninety percent of the time, it is my main sinker that is under or behind that log or rock, NOT my hook itself! Someone, somewhere, back when I had hair (a long time ago) taught me that a pinch-on sinker beats a barrel swivel hands down as a way to keep your heavier lead away from your hook. Obviously we do not want the sinker banging up against the hook and that is why we must separate them. 99% of fishermen use the barrel swivel, less than 1% of us use the split-shot, and WE ARE RIGHT and THEY ARE WRONG!

Some people use egg-shaped sinkers, as I do, and others prefer a wide variety of shapes,"bait-walker," as Dan Gapen calls them, or bank, pyramid, dipsey/bell, etc. Some Englishmen like to use a very long thin lead that, like an egg/barrel, has a hole running straight through it. Again, every photo that I have seen in every publication still shows the sinker, whatever variation is being used, stopped by that two-way barrel swivel.

The operative word here is STOPPED. If your weight is stuck under a branch and a swivel is in use, a tug of war ensues. This gets particularly crazy when a big carp is at the other end of the short leader, a foot or two past the branch. They often do not wait to see who wins, angler, or wood/rock, and break you off with a lurch forward.

THE DIFFERENCE

If you stop your sinker a foot or two above the hook with a split shot, and you get hung, again, more often than not it is the sinker that is stuck, not your hook. If a barrel swivel is used, luck alone will get the whole deal back to you. Tug until it all gets released, or until you break the line at your barrel swivel knot. You can move from side to side, twang the line like a banjo to try and free it up, etc. Most times, it simply becomes a tug of war. IF the line is fairly light test, the rock or tree usually wins. That is with a swivel.

If you are using a split shot, and your sinker, shot and hook are on the other side of the hang-up, a straight pull forward will cause the egg sinker to slide forward pushing the pinch-on, because it is NOT an immovable object as a swivel is. Even if the pinch-on is on tight, it will still slide to the hook and most of the time, this action will cause the sinker to dislodge itself as it rides to the hook.

When you get everything back to shore, slide the egg and split shot back up the line and clamp the shot back before rebaiting and casting out again.

If your hook itself tethered to the bottom, luck alone will release you but if the sinker is causing the snag, as is usually the case, the pinch-on is the difference. Wherever you are reading this book, and no matter how wonderfully prepared you are with rod-pods, electronic bite indicators, bivvies, bait-runner reels and the like, this simple thought can make the rest of your carp fishing life much better.

My guess is that the British hair-rig using Carper who does not bait his hook itself may get the bare hook into bottom more than I have done because my hook is protected by bait. That fellow too will still get his sinker under the snag many times more than his hook.

FISH-FINDER RIGS

Fellows who like to attach chumming devices of one manner or another above the sinker can still do this when rigging with barrel sinker and pinch-on. Here a small hollow tube with loop on it, called a "Fish-finder" rig, is all you need. Put your reel line through the egg sinker, and then through the hollow tube, and tie your hook on — with or without a hair-rig. Back the egg sinker and fish-finder tube up, say 15 inches, and then clamp your split-shot on. Now tie into the fish-finder loop whatever kind of device you want, with lighter line. This leader will hold your chum pod, etc., and still break away if that is what hangs you up.

CHAPTER 23

How To Do It

ROD PLACEMENT

Whether fishing from shore or boat, most Carpers agree that it is very important to have your rods resting parallel to the water. In America, most anglers like to have rod tip high and reel low, but I never thought that this made sense at all. Yes, if your drag is too tight by mistake this gives you the chance of grabbing the outfit before a fish pulls it into the drink. Some of the lowliest of fish are capable of taking your rod for a one-way swim, unless you follow the simple style we will talk about in a while.

Guys who put the butt down on land or boat floor and have the tip facing skyward are doing it all wrong. The rod held in this manner will bounce in any kind of wind or current at all, and create unnatural movement to the bait at the other end. In particular for carp, no motion is the best motion, unless you are controlling your bait's motion in a downstream or downwind roll.

WIND-WIGGLES

The elevated rod tip flipping in the air will not only create movement that could scare carp away, after staring at it for a while, you will start to see what I call "WIND-WIGGLES."

Watch that tip minutes on end and you will swear that the movement of the rod will not be caused by a breeze or current but rather than by the start of a bite. The wiggle is not Mr. Man, it is your mind playing tricks with you.

Flat to the water is key to really keep from scaring fish away as well as reducing your false bite readings.

FROM SHORE
ROD-PODS

A stake-out system, involving a contraption that involves six to nine metal poles that either stick into the ground at shore, or at least rest on land on little feet, is a great way to go. This outfit involves snag-bars, buzzer bars, and who knows what else to present a group of offerings to waiting carp offshore. We have talked of these methods at length in our chapter about England but make no mistake about it, they do it far better than we do in America.

The bottom line is that they are trying to position two to three rods parallel to the water with this rig and at the same time, have electronic bite-indicators in place on each of the rods to assist in shouting the alarm, signaling that Mr. Man is sniffing around. The scream of a drag works best, but if the angler is asleep in his comfy tent (bivvie) the bite-indicator is sure to snap him straight upright.

FORKED STICK

A bit cheaper by far than the Rod-Pod is the use of a couple of forked sticks, found on the ground, or created by breaking a dead branch or two off of a nearby tree. A garden stake that has an open loop on top is fancier, but the basic premise is still the same.

Plant the stick or stake in the ground as deeply as you can and have the top fork only six to twelve inches up. Place your rod into the crook of the stick and you are almost ready. If you were not careful, you could have placed your line down into the fork under the rod. With drag wide open, you still may have created a mess, because the weight of the rod will nail the line to the crook and prevent the fish from taking line on his run. I have seen quite a few rods catapulted skywards this way!

The solution is very simple. Carefully lift your line away from the fork and place it on one side or another of same, then putting the rod back into the crook. This way a fish can run with ease, and your line will follow. You do need to be careful though when lifting the rod, so that you do not tangle the line back into the stick. If in current or wind, always place the line on the down-

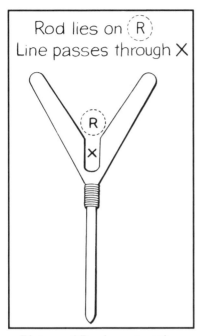

Rod lies on (R)
Line passes through X

R

X

Picture of Dan's contraption,
taken out of his book.

wind or down-current side of the stick or stake for best results.

Dan Gapen illustrates a forked metal rod in his book that has an open area beneath the fork that your line can run through with no difficulty. I suppose these are easy to make and are certainly logical to use.

The key still is to have the rod down low. Propping it up ever so little on your tackle box or on a low rock will work too. Fancy is not always necessary.

FROM A BOAT

Placing a rod down in your boat the wrong way could cost you that rod, in a heartbeat, if a Big-Scaler takes off quickly. For openers, let's again stick to the same basic thought as fishing from shore. Have the rod rest parallel to the water. This cuts down on getting hung up on floating weeds, as well as reduces the wind-wiggles, etc.

My boat has no rod holders, either for riding or to be used while fishing. That is intentional, to cut down on the number of problems I would otherwise get while working to double anchor the boat. Rod holders that face the water may hold a rod well, if perfectly placed, but if not, some rods have been seen to leap out of a boat, as a torpedo may do.

The key here is to rest the rod down, across the gunnels if your rod is long, or at least have the tip-end on one gunnel and the butt on an object in the boat. That object could be your tackle box, camera bag, etc., what is critical is that the rod butt, NOT the reel, is resting. If your reel is laying on something, that could keep your drag from releasing line. The placement is critical for this reason. At all times, keep the reel from touching anything when you put the outfit down.

I suppose that my boats, first, "The Karp Katcher," and then the three "Gone Fishin's," have produced at least 1,000 carp, and I never had a rod taken into the drink that I put down. There was one silly time that I actually had a slippery rod pulled out of my hand, to tell the truth. That reel had open drag and after casting another outfit a half-dozen times I actually caught my line, and wound up retrieving everything, including the 5 pounder that caused my mistake to occur.

DEPTH-FINDERS

Also called Fish-Locaters, by whatever name, they do help. Most carp fishing involves water that is twenty feet deep or less, so looking on your scope and "reading" fish is not easy in such shallow water. I have seen carp this way, but much of my hunting is for drop-offs, not for fish.

The use of a depth-finder, reading where changes in depth take place, is a fine way to improve your results. In current, anchor over shallower water and fish into a deeper spot. Not easy to do, but with enough practice in double anchoring, you can do it. You do need to move in quiet though, and here is where oars or an electric motor is the way to go to avoid scaring fish away.

You can also fish into deeper holes in calm water, simply by "reading" the water before you set your anchors.

METHODS OF BAITING

No, not chumming, baiting. Be it on your hook itself, the old fashioned way, or on a hair-rig, nearly all people seem to try and attract as well as feed. Carpworld published a photo of a mess of stuff resting at bottom, containing three or four boilie freebies, several more hooked onto a hair rig, and a huge mass of paste on a chum mixer. This could drive a confused carp to the psychiatrists couch, not knowing what to eat first. Chumming itself has been adequately discussed but the subject now is the hook bait.

WITH FLOTATION

In spite of my excellent luck in catching carp, I must now admit to having never taken carp off of bottom. Again, talking about Dan Gapen, and the many experts in England, some folks use, for example, two kernels of corn, followed by a small piece of plastic, in the same size and shape as the kernel, then followed by two more kernels. This could be on your hook itself, or on a hair-rig. The idea is that the plastic floats your kernels upward where some carp may be swimming. It also makes it easier to see, especially if the bottom is muddy or covered with weed.

Use of a miniature marshmallow instead of the styrofoam or other plastic may be even better because a carp may want to eat the marshmallow instead. If you take a kid with you Carping, make sure to have some extra "bait" though, because they could sneak it all away. The 47 pound New Jersey State Record carp that was caught in 1995 ate a Berkeley Power Bait nugget, intended for trout. This nugget, as with marshmallow, etc., floats!

A mad scientist somewhere created a simple little device that allows you to put a large worm on, and then stick a hollow pin into the worm and blow air into the poor wiggler. This will float the worm up off bottom, causing it to dance by itself. Someone should report this to the A.S.P.C.W. (American Society for the Prevention of Cruelty to Worms.)

BAIT SHAPE

Boilie, doughball or Mommah-Liggah, most people like to create their baits in the shape of a ball. Personally, again, based on years of experience, I really much prefer that my bait is pear-shaped. I want the fish to suck in the larger end of the "pear," so that is how I face the bait on my hook. Now that I will try the hair-rig method also, I will again have the top of the pear up on top of the rig.

If you are using particles such as berries or corn, this is a no-brainer. Using a worm is easy too, do it the same way as you would do for any other fish. Try to not use a long snake-length worm that is only hooked one time though. That is both too easy for the carp to get off without being hooked, and it also entices far too many other fish to eat. There you may be, with no bait at all and not knowing it.

I like to hook a worm through the top of the head and out the collar, then penetrating the worm again once about half way down to its tail.

DAY VS. NIGHT

There is something far more exciting about night fishing than fishing during daylight, and for a single person especially. Somehow a statement to your better half that you are going Carping all night long could not be taken well. As discussed previously, daylight hours are as good as or better for much of the year in the northeastern United States, but in summertime, sometimes night time is the only time. You just need to prepare better for night.

To fish at night, you need at least two flashlights (torches), because you surely will lose one right away if you only bring one. Have an extra supply of batteries with you as well. A lantern — kerosene or propane, is good to have if legal to use where you will be fishing.

As a kid, we used to light fires at our campsite, again, only doing so if legal, and some of the best meals I ever ate came cooked over these fires. Cooking a fresh batch of corn meal bait this way was also a nice thing to do.

Some people think that shining your light on the water may scare carp away, so do try to avoid doing so. What is helpful is to leave a flashlight on at all times, propped up in an angle so that it illuminates all of your rods, from side to side, not facing the water. This light reduces the otherwise critical need for some manner of "night guide," bits of paper or little aluminum cup and clip combinations that are on your rod to signal a bite before drag or bite-indicators do their thing.

Night fishing usually requires at least two people so that if one fellow is asleep, the other could grab a throbbing rod. If working carefully, the awake angler might even be able to catch a fish on the other guy's line and swear that it was on his own for the record keepers. Do try to have a cooler full of food with you for night fishing, and a thermos of hot coffee, tea or chocolate. Pizza delivery trucks do not generally go out into the woods in the middle of the night to make a delivery!

OPEN OR CLOSED BALE

Clearly, if you can fish with bale open, this is tops. In a lake or slow moving river, cast out, take the floating line in, and put the rod down, with bale open, and drag partially closed. You may need to hold a coil or two of line down to the ground with a little extra piece of cooked corn meal or maybe a tiny twig. When Mr. Man takes your bait and runs, you need no bite indicator, if your eyes are open and you are looking at the line. The bait or twig will leap skyward and your line will literally melt off the reel, with coils flowing out in a whoosh. What a happy moment that is. What a great number of Carpers who fall down from excitement as they try to bend down to pick the rod up!

If you have the chance to fish with open bale, fine, but do remember that with bale closed, you must either own a tackle store filled with many rods and reels, be independently wealthy and not care about losing gear from the bite, or remember to open the drag.

WEIGHT OR NOT

Once more, a subject referred to earlier, but still worth repeating. Simply put, the best weight is your bait, period! A carp that sees one object to eat and has nothing else in the way, no weight, swivel, or other device, will go after such an offering with less fear. Placing your baited hair-rig or a baited hook itself in a "Margin" (a spot close to shore that requires no casting weight) is truly the best.

Some people like to fish the Margin with a very long fibreglass pole and no reel at all, and others go with the standby spinning gear. Either way, you can put your bait in front of the face of a carp this way and it is a fine style to go with. There are people who blindly fish this way and other who actually stalk a fish they see. The fish could be seen swimming or digging bottom. Either way, a slam that occurs only ten to twenty feet from where you stand is a slam of major impact into your shoulder socket as you rear back!

In still water, or if barely moving, a large Boilie, Mommah-Liggah ball, or hunk of par-cooked potato by itself can be cast well offshore and once more, without anything else on, bites come more often.

That 12 pounder I told you about catching in a slow moving section of the Walkill River with a fly rod and reel loaded with only monofiliment was caught on a corn meal ball and no weight.

WAIT OR NOT
(OR WHEN TO PULL THE TRIGGER)

Okay, you did it all right. You cast out, took in nearly all of the slack line, and properly placed your rod down, parallel to the water, and you wait, and wait, and wait! Ten minutes or two hours may pass by, and suddenly, the wait ends, and the excitement begins.

It could be a sudden and wild drag tear, or maybe just the hello pecking of a careful carp. Get ready, because fun lies just ahead, at the edge of the water, where Mr. Man is preparing to do battle with you. Are you ready?

Keeping the drag wide open, pick the rod up, with tip-top pointed towards the water, making no movement at all take place to your rod tip, or to the line itself. Whether the fish is screaming away or just tapping, do NOT pull the trigger yet.

Some people like to respond by whacking the rod into a fish that is hitting with a staccato beat, thinking the hook is already in the mouth of their opponent. Frankly, I wait for straight, smooth swimming first.

When Mr. Man is swimming away, quickly or at a slow gait, you should gently lift the rod tip high, without letting the fish feel you. If you have had an open bale in quiet water, this is easier to do. If with bale closed and drag open, you can still do this, pulling line out of the reel as you lift the tip but you will need more caution to avoid scaring the fish. A little slack is needed to keep the fish from disappearing.

With rod tip high and bale now closed, and drag (brake) still loose, let the fish bend the rod tip towards the water and place an index finger on the reel spool to stop the line from going out and, at the same time, PULL THE TRIGGER! Slam that steel into the fishes mouth, and take your finger off the spool instantly so that line can be taken, or else you will break the line-or rather, Ole Puckerpuss will do so.

If you let the fish move, and bend the rod, and do everything we just said, you will stick the hook into at least 75% of each carp that is running. This will occur with bait on a hook, and maybe with an even higher hit ratio if using a hair-rig.

CHAPTER 24

Release Alive

A wide swing is occurring in America, from destruction to an attempt at proper respect. This has been going on for many years in Great Britain already, but the majority of American's still would rather see carp piled up dead, like cords of wood.

#!"HUNTERS"#!

We still hear about the Robin Hood type who goes out with bow and arrow, bent on blowing a hole in the side of a bunch of carp. If the goal was food, I suppose I could live with that, but most of the clowns who kill carp in this manner just throw the poor beasts away dead or dying after getting their arrows out.

Rarely are carp that are shot by arrows even considered for food, for the "hunter" or even for a poor person that the hunter may know of.

Perhaps one day we may see this type of slaughter made illegal in the United States. Hopefully, my fellow members of The Carp Anglers Group and I will work together in the near future to try to get such legislation passed.

Forgetting such so-called "Sportsmen," let us get to the purpose of this chapter, discussion on "Catch & Release."

TOURNAMENTS

English Carpers will sometimes hold their carp alive in the water at shore in a very large but soft mesh bag. If contained this way and adequate space is allowed to keep them from suffocating, I suppose that this is okay, but I still would prefer to see every carp put right back to freedom after giving an angler a valiant battle. Yes, tournaments often require aggregate weight of live fish and such containment may be one good way to handle things, but I do not personally have any interest in such events.

Bass Tournaments in the states are most popular and folks keep a bunch of bass alive in their boat's live-bait wells. This should work too for carp, if enough space exists. Since most carp fishing in England is done from shore, that fairly well eliminates that style, but stateside, that is another issue.

Use of fish stringers, placed through the mouth and out a gill, or as bad, through the nose hole, may give an angler the appearance of allowing him to release his catch alive, but virtually all such fish will die shortly from the damage caused by the stringer. The thrashing alone of the fish will tear them up horribly.

My brother Murray sent me a copy of a story he clipped out the *Wall Street Journal* in October of 1995 in which the writer was talking about what I call "Fish-Right's Activist's." Among other bits of silliness written about in the story was revelation of the fact that "In England, underwater saboteurs in scuba gear have prowled the deep at fishing tournaments, herding away trophy carp and snipping off lures."

I really do believe in "Save-the Whale's," and release most of all fish that I catch alive, but the people of Clapham Commons in South London who tried to prohibit all fishing in their largest pond, to prevent cruelty to fish, no doubt, went a bit too far. You see, tournaments gather publicity and some members of the public get carried away.

SAFE RELEASE

Releasing a carp alive is somewhat simple, if a specific procedure is followed. Most carp do not swallow a hook, and you can usually see the bend of the hook right at the fishes lip.

If the hook is not visible, and I may have caught ten or so carp in my lifetime that did swallow a hook, that is where a good pair of scissors come in. Little nail clippers, a sharp knife, perhaps a single edged razor blade, or anything that can quickly cut your line will do. Just bring the fish close and cut, without taking its head out of the water at all.

A WORD FROM KODAK

Many people love to take a picture with their carp before releasing them. Again, the British are way ahead of American's. They buy carp blankets, and no, not to tuck a fish in nightie, nightie, this is done to hold a carp so that no damage can occur to its body. Some of these blankets are padded for even more gentle handling.

Virtually every photo that I have seen of a carp caught in Great Britain involved an angler holding the carp by their body, with one hand behind the head and the second hand in front of the tail. This gives the fish the least amount of chance at getting damaged. This is the best way to record your catch for posterity, and give the fish the best chance at survival.

Way back when, many fishermen who had no desire at all to keep a carp would still hold the fish under a gill for the camera-man. This did make for a secure hold, but it also tore the gill more often than not. As the carp struggled, its own weight would cause a tear to take place and blood would follow. How many of these carp survived is not certain, but you can wager that many died a slow death from the damage caused.

I used to hold a carp by its lip, or put my fingers into their eye sockets for the photo album. These methods too must have caused some damage.

A GOOD CHANCE OF SURVIVAL

My gear includes a good-sized net that has a built in scale in its handle. This is one way to get a good weight without touching the fish. Lift the net out of the water, read the scale, remove the hook and put the fish and net back in the water. Gently turn the net over and watch your happy fish swim away, not much worse for the experience.

There are soft-mesh nets available that can lift a carp gently. The net and contents can then be weighed with an accurate scale. The angler knows the weight of the empty but wet net so true weight of each fish is easy to determine.

AGAIN, SAFE RELEASE

I still would rather have nothing touch the carp because some protective slime may be removed, whether it be by net, "blankie," or hand.

The only true and proven way to guaranty the best chance of "Mr. Man" living to fight another day is to not touch the fish at all. Take the fish to shore or to the side of your boat and remove the hook with a long pair of pliers or forceps, if you can see the hook, or simply cut the line at the mouth.

Lifting a fish out of the water with your rod tip, even a tiny bit, can cause damage so, again, forceps, pliers, or snip!

"Catch and Release" ... the best way to say THANK YOU to each carp for giving you so very much enjoyment and pleasure.

CHAPTER 25

That Sweet Sound

There are many sounds that I like to hear. Near the top of the list of course are the words, "I love you," but you have to do something or at least had to have done something to earn those words, be it from a parent, spouse, lover, child or grandchild.

Another sound is the splash of a carp, or from a bunch of them. Whether they are spawning, feeding or just playing around, the kerplunk of a carp in the middle of the night can really crank my juices up, big time.

The best sound to hear, if you are really after a truly selfish experience, is the sound of your own reel, screaming off drag. With brake protesting in vain, and line melting away, even though this has happened to me time after time, my knees do turn to a'knockin'!

That sweet sound, DRAG, followed up by an equally fine one, the sound of a safely released carp, swimming away, to give me even more pleasure next time — YES!

Scuze me, gone fishin'.